PRESIDENTIAL
DOODLES

PRESIDENTIAL DOODLES

TWO CENTURIES OF SCRIBBLES,
SCRATCHES, SQUIGGLES & SCRAWLS
FROM THE OVAL OFFICE

FROM THE CREATORS OF **CABINET MAGAZINE**

TEXT AND INTRODUCTION BY **DAVID GREENBERG**
FOREWORD BY **PAUL COLLINS**

BASIC BOOKS
A MEMBER OF THE PERSEUS BOOKS GROUP
New York

Designed by Carole Goodman / Blue Anchor Design

Library of Congress Cataloging-in-Publication Data
A CIP for this book is available from the Library of Congress.
10 ISBN 0–465–03266–4
13 ISBN 978–0–465–03266–2
06 07 08 / 10 9 8 7 6 5 4 3 2 1

THERE ARE MANY THINGS THAT WE WOULD
THROW AWAY IF WE WERE NOT AFRAID THAT
OTHERS MIGHT PICK THEM UP.

—OSCAR WILDE

✳

FOREWORD

DOODLER-IN-CHIEF

PAUL COLLINS

Decisions, decisions.

Decisions . . . decisions . . . decisions.

THE WORD IS WRITTEN SEVENTEEN TIMES OVER BY JOHN F. KENNEDY—
"underlined, boxed in, and crossed out" as a reporter noted—on a yellow legal
pad in 1961, not long after he took office. Actually, the word is misspelled
seventeen times over as "decesions," but no matter . . . who would ever see it?
Millions, as it turned out: In the wake of Kennedy's assassination, a collection of
his doodles, which included sailboats, underlined words, and overlapping boxes,
went on a memorial tour of twenty-three cities in the summer of 1964. The
exhibit attracted throngs of visitors; they solemnly filed past, eager to view the
simple remains of a complex life.

It was not always thus; for although not impossible, one cannot very easily
doodle with, say, a sharpened goose feather. Writing with a quill is a delib-
erative task. First, you must painstakingly cut your quill: take a sharp
penknife and use its blade back to scrape the quill's surface; and then, using
the blade edge, cut a sharp, angled nib with a small and precise slit in the
middle. A slip of the blade, and you'll need to start all over again—or, perhaps,
get yourself a bandage. All this rather takes the fun out of scribbling googly-eyed

faces, lazy spirals, and appallingly disproportionate dogs that sport gigantic rows of teeth.

And so you begin to see why there are not too many Founding Doodlers.

Even a properly sharpened quill is damnably difficult to write with: it is inconsistent, it needs constant dipping, and it dulls quickly. The labor of quill writing meant that an eighteenth-century meeting required a secretary to take notes: others were not expected to trouble themselves with writing, and the secretary was certainly not allowed to doodle. Today, however, Washington teems with meetings at which every person in attendance has their own pen and paper. We can loop endless circles without spilling or running out of ink, indeed without looking down at what we are doing. Even this happy state of modern affairs couldn't always be taken for granted: back in 1959, the first American manufacturer of ballpoints found a public so wary that, to make the ultramodern device seem more reassuringly familiar, it had to disguise ballpoints as pencils by encasing them in wood.

In fact, three things needed to happen before doodling could become, if not the Sport of Kings, at least the Fidget of Presidents. The first was the invention of the steel-nibbed pen. Like any terribly useful invention, nobody can quite agree on its origins. One of the earliest accounts places a steel pen in the hand of a certain Peregrine Williamson, a Baltimore jeweler in the first few years of the 1800s. Peregrine was terrible at cutting quills; in desperation, he contrived a sort of steel quill that would never need sharpening. He didn't keep his jerry-rigged contraption to himself for long, though: soon, he was making $600 a month from his invention. By 1823, the Englishman James Perry was mass-producing them, and a new generation of children learned to write with the newfangled metal quill. "The Metallic pen is in the ascendant, and the glory of goosedom has departed forever," one textbook stated flatly.

But then there's the matter of paper. Paper was manufactured from old rags, and by the age of the steel pen, demand was outstripping the national supply of used underwear and grubby bonnets: paper was expensive, and not the sort of thing you'd waste on aimless scribbles. Everything from hay to hemp was tried out as a substitute material, with mixed results at best. It took the German inventor Friedrich Keller, in 1843, to develop the first recognizably modern process for mass-producing paper out of ground wood pulp. The resulting product was easily shipped via burgeoning rail systems. Soon, paper was abundant; it was sold by the pad, the memo book, and the sheaf.

Writing itself became looser and more doodle-like. Itinerant penmanship instructors, often juggling other fashionable sidelines in daguerreotyping and cutting silhouettes, distinguished themselves in the mid-1800s with manuals featuring ever-more baroque swirls and flourishes, not to mention fanciful drawings of angels, birds, and grinning fish; indeed, the title page of at least one textbook is so covered with this calligraphic frippery that the words themselves are obliterated. But by the time of Abraham Lincoln, a generation of children had grown up with increasingly affordable pencils and steel pens. These youngsters practiced flourishes, repeated words over and over, and sketched out fanciful beasts in cheap notebooks and on the endpapers of Latin grammars—and, just as their schoolmasters had claimed, a few would grow up to be president.

* * * *

Republicans are the greatest doodlers.

Now before any Democrat takes offense, it may console them to know that in nineteenth-century parlance a "doodler" was also a corrupt politician. But when it comes to conventional figurative drawing, Republican presidents do hold a clear lead: they *can* draw Tippy the Turtle, and they *did* draw the Pirate. Reagan often handed out his correspondence-course-style drawings as prizes at meetings; the Eisenhower administration was so fond of paint-by-numbers kits that an aide prodded the cabinet and visitors into creating a *de facto* White House gallery of kitsch. (The Eisenhower Library's paint-by-the-numbers collection includes *Swiss Village,* painted by J. Edgar Hoover, and *Old Mill,* painted by Ethel Merman.) And Herbert Hoover was so well-known for his ornate geometrical patterns that autograph dealers were already scooping them up while he was still in office. In 1930, one collector even copied some of Hoover's patterns onto fabric and unveiled a line of "Hoover Scribble Rompers" for young children.

Other White House doodles were not so openly exhibited, for the notion that a doodle gives insight into a troubled psyche had quite a vogue in the mid-twentieth century. Aides to Secretary of State John Foster Dulles were instructed to carefully gather up his many doodles after meetings, lest they reveal a psychological insight to spies. But then, Dulles also knew that a well-placed doodle can be a weapon. He infuriated Soviet foreign minister Molotov during negotiations by doodling constantly and by his habit of pointedly pausing to sharpen his pencil with a knife. It was no less disconcerting when an American negotiator noticed Josef Stalin idly using a red pencil to draw hearts with little question marks inside.

And although presidential doodles have managed to stay clear of trouble, other doodling in the White House can cause the occasional sticky situation. Attorney General Elliott Richardson not only irritated Richard Nixon by his doodling–"He thought I wasn't paying attention," the former *Harvard Lampoon* cartoonist explained–he very nearly scotched his own cabinet nomination by doodling through his confirmation hearings, causing senators to accuse him of arrogance. Hugh Johnson, FDR's Depression-era head of the National Recovery Administration, was caught scratching the word "HELL" into his memo pad during one press conference; more recently, the baroquely doodled notes of George W. Bush's speechwriter Michael Gerson have also raised eyebrows. "If these ever become part of the Presidential records," the *New York Times* quoted

Karl Rove joking to Gerson, "future historians will say that some deranged person was near the President."

Indeed.

But what *do* doodles mean? Although some have appreciated Hoover's doodles, for instance, for their purely visual qualities—in 1968, the painter Lois Thayer actually exhibited twenty-five canvases based on Hoover's scratch pads—others have tried to divine his personality from them. In 1982, *Time* magazine submitted presidential doodles to a "graphologist," who opined that Hoover was "the most confused" president, while an attempt by the *New York Times* in 1947 saw *their* expert deeming Hoover "feverishly active and well-organized." Not to be outdone, London newspapers recently pounced on a paper left on Prime Minister Tony Blair's table after an economic summit; they hired graphologists, and even a clairvoyant, and smugly announced that Blair's doodles revealed him to be mentally unstable, impractical, and unable to finish tasks. Unfortunately, their combined expertise failed to notice that the doodle didn't belong to Blair, Bush, or to any other head of state at all. The allegedly ineffectual and hazy-minded doodler turned out to be the software billionaire Bill Gates—a fellow who, one gathers, can doodle whatever he likes.

Doodles rarely reveal clear insight into a person beyond what is immediately on their mind. In 1942, the American Institute of Laundering announced that a survey of commercial laundries found that restaurant tablecloths had been pressed into wartime doodle service by civilians, as "90 percent of doodling on tablecloths today is concerned with war strategy" in the form of crudely drawn maps and arrows. "Laundry operators are not over-impressed with the brilliance of the strategy shown by the doodlers," one report dryly noted. And yet such obvious planning is noticeably absent from presidential doodles: their very ordinariness is a cipher.

Perhaps this is why doodles are so compelling. If they are significant, it is not because they are great art or the products of great men. It is because they are ordinary, and historians have fought to preserve open-access laws so that presidential doodles can be so ordinary. Anyone can view them–*they belong to us*. And when we view them, we see that they resemble our own words and our own idle lines. The drawing or scrawled comment on a yellow pad is like an ancient cave painting: a familiar image, but from an unimaginable distance of time and situation.

INTRODUCTION:
PRESIDENTIAL DOODLES: A BRIEF HISTORY

DAVID GREENBERG

SOON AFTER SOMALI MILITIAMEN KILLED EIGHTEEN AMERICAN SOLDIERS in Mogadishu on October 3, 1993, President Clinton convened his national security team in the White House. As recalled by the counterterrorism expert Richard Clarke, the president sat silently as his aides reviewed the situation. Then, Clarke wrote, "When they had talked themselves out, Clinton stopped doodling and looked up. 'Okay, here's what we're going to do.'"[1]

Apart from the atypical decisiveness Clarke attributes to Clinton, what strikes the reader in this passage is that amid the most severe international crisis of his tenure to that point, the leader of the free world was, of all things, *doodling*. We imagine meetings of the National Security Council to be efficiently run affairs where matters of the utmost gravity are discussed; we don't expect the president to be dithering, daydreaming, or making little drawings. But here, while Warren Christopher, Les Aspin, and Colin Powell held forth about matters of global consequence, the commander-in-chief was scratching out idle marks on a pad of paper. What makes it more interesting, the activity wasn't evidence of dereliction of duty, a sign that he wasn't paying attention. On the contrary, in Clarke's telling, it indicated supreme confidence: Clinton could afford to doodle because he already knew what had to be done.

Clarke isn't the only writer to use the image of a high official scribbling away to achieve dramatic effect. The historian Herbert S. Parmet writes of the cool contempt that Secretary of State John Foster Dulles showed to his British counterpart, Anthony Eden, in the 1950s: "It must . . . have galled Eden to address Dulles while the American doodled on an ever-present legal-sized yellow pad, only glancing upward occasionally and rather quizzically . . . as though the forthcoming words were perfectly predictable." Eisenhower's science adviser, George Kistiakowsky, wrote of how the president himself, on hearing an aide discuss the mounting danger posed by the Soviet Union, "quite suddenly stopped his usual doodling, raised a hand, and said: 'Please enter a minority report of one.'" John F. Kennedy was, according to Peter Edelman, a former aide to Robert Kennedy, "doodling 'poverty' on a yellow legal pad at the last cabinet meeting before he died." In some cases doodles—or their near kin—have entered political lore. Supply-side apostle Arthur Laffer scrawled on a cocktail napkin the chart that would guide Reaganomics. Reagan's aide Pat Buchanan later got in trouble by jotting "succumbing to the pressure of the Jews" over and over in a meeting about whether to scuttle the president's visit to a Nazi graveyard. George W. Bush scrawled "not on my watch" on a memo about the Rwandan genocide—words used against him as Sudanese were slaughtered in Darfur.[2]

The image of a president doodling can have all kinds of effects. It may jar us through its juxtaposition of high-stakes drama and mundane habit. It may disturb us by exposing the world's most powerful man's childish side (Reagan drew babies and horses). It may shock us by suggesting a contempt on the doodler's part for the interlocutors he's ignoring. Or it may delight us to see how an offhand note can poetically express what reams of formal communication could not.

Whatever their particular effects, there's no denying that presidential doodles are intriguing. The question is why.

* * * *

Doodling is an ancient habit. Prehistoric South African cave drawings and Mesopotamian clay tablets bear errant marks unrelated to their main subject matter. Yet only in the twentieth century was the word *doodle* used to denote an absentminded scribble and people began to study the form. And the most popular prism of interpretation has been the psychoanalytic, as aficionados scrutinized doodles for the insights they may offer into the unconscious thoughts lurking in the recesses of the artist's psyche.[3]

The first person to recognize–or at least to cash in on–this now-familiar notion was a colorful mid-twentieth-century character named Russell M. Arundel. Born in 1902, Arundel worked as a journalist and Capitol Hill staffer in Washington in the 1920s and 1930s. He showed an early interest in the images of presidents when he served on the Mount Rushmore Memorial Commission. Later, as a lobbyist for the sugar industry, he developed a friendship with Senator Joseph R. McCarthy and was hauled before a Senate committee for signing over a $20,000 check to McCarthy, allegedly as a loan. In 1949, Arundel achieved still more notoriety by purchasing a small island off the coast of Nova Scotia, naming it the "Principality of Outer Baldonia" (even though it remained part of Canada) and nearly provoking hostilities with the Soviet Union. He spent his final decades running a Pepsi-Cola subsidiary and serving as a leading figure in the Virginia fox-hunting scene.[4]

For all these feats, Arundel's most precious achievement may be his 1937 book, *Everybody's Pixillated*, a compilation of doodles by famous figures, including Cab Calloway, Helen Hayes, Huey Long, and the Duke of Windsor. (The volume also contained an impressive selection of doodles by presidents, some of which appear in this book, but apart from the inimitable Herbert Hoover, the most proficient presidential doodlers–Eisenhower, Kennedy, Johnson, and Reagan– came to office after Arundel's fancy had turned to steeplechasing.) Arundel grasped the nature of the modern instinct for doodling. "Place a pencil and pad near the telephone of any human of more than primeval intelligence and the bet is ten to one that he'll doodle during his next telephone call," he wrote in *Everybody's Pixillated*. "Whether teamster or genius, he will produce triangles, circles, arrows, mice, stars or some other penciled designs and tie them together in a pattern which mightily resembles surrealism in a lunatic asylum."[5]

For all his acuity and measured whimsy, Arundel was in the grip of a pop Freudianism that still pervaded American culture in the 1930s. As W. H. Auden wrote a few years later, Freud had become "no more a person/Now a whole climate of opinion." His work influenced filmmakers and sociologists, poets and policy analysts. It made sense, of course, to regard the doodle as a relative of the Freudian slip or the verbal free association–an articulation of repressed truth unleashed by the unconscious while the ego was looking the other way. Doodles, as Arundel put it, "are psychic blueprints of man's inner thoughts and emotions that have slipped from the deeps of memory onto paper." Accordingly, he interpreted the doodles in his book as revealing aspects of their authors' personalities. He even included in the book a ten-page "Pixillation Chart," featuring 120 common doodles and corresponding thumbnail analyses so that readers could probe their own psyches as well as those of the celebrities whose jottings Arundel had culled.[6]

This Freudian approach to doodle interpretation has since held sway. A 1947 article in the *New York Times Magazine* that reprinted samples from Arundel's collection concluded that in doodles "the subconscious may yield a great store of dreams, fancies, inspirations–and even the most carefully guarded fact." A 1982 *Time* magazine feature on presidential doodles took a similar line.[7]

There were, however, dissenters from this dominant wisdom. Norman R. Uris, the author of a 1970 doodle compilation, was resolutely anti-analytical in contemplating the drawings he gathered from such celebrities as Betty Grable and Julian Bond. "To me, doodling is an art form and is no more or less symbolic than the work of any artist," Uris asserted. "Doodles may be interesting, but you can't judge what or who a person is–or isn't–by looking at his doodle."[8]

Still, you don't have to turn the doodle into the key to the unconscious to realize that it's not just any ordinary drawing. Doodles are practically *sui generis* (especially among presidential communications) because they aren't meant for anyone else to see. As UN Undersecretary General Ralph Bunche replied when Uris asked him for a contribution to his book: "To do a doodle to order would really be faking, because a doodle ought to be spontaneous and subconscious. In fact, since receiving your letter, I have found that my doodling is spoiled because the letter has made me self-conscious about it." (Other luminaries also rejected Uris's request for doodles, though most did so on less principled grounds. "I must confess, I don't know what is a 'doodle.' I did not find this word in the *Oxford Concise Dictionary,*" replied Israeli Prime Minister David Ben-Gurion. "Will you explain to me what is a doodle?")[9]

For all those who declined to help, Uris was able to secure a doodle from President Richard Nixon–a particularly impressive feat because Nixon had declined (through his aide H. R. Haldeman) to give one to his own speechwriter, William Safire, who was also a collector. Perhaps Nixon, who had a lot to hide, was afraid that psychologists would try to read his unconscious; despite his outward loathing of them, Nixon actually had a strong penchant for thinking psychoanalytically. On one occasion he admitted that he tried to decipher other people's doodles. "I always watch my opposite numbers to see how they doodle," Nixon told his ghostwriter Frank Gannon in a post-presidential interview. "I draw squares and diamonds and that sort of thing. . . . [I'm] probably a square doodler," he confessed, in a clever if unintentional pun. Nixon continued: "I noticed that, for example, in 1972, when we were having our first discussion with Brezhnev about missiles. We–the argument was as to whether or not a big missile could be put in a smaller hole. . . . While we were talking about it, he would draw holes and then missiles . . . to see whether or not they could go in the holes and so forth and so on. And down here, when we were meeting in a cabaña looking out over the Black Sea, he doodled–in this case, he drew a heart with an arrow through it. I don't know what that signified, but that was when we were failing to reach agreement on a proposal to limit [nuclear warheads], which we had proposed and which they had rejected."[10]

Nixon, unfortunately, didn't develop his interpretation of Brezhnev's artwork. Yet it's less the meaning he might have ascribed to his counterpart's doodle that merits note than the very instinct to interpret it at all. Not that Nixon's propensity is so unusual: despite the dissenting strain that insists on seeing doodles (and slips of the tongue) as innocent of meaning, the impulse to read doodles psychoanalytically remains all but irresistible. These days it pops up in women's and teenage girls' magazines. "Discover What Your Doodles Say About You," promises a headline in *Mademoiselle*. "Doodles & Squiggles: What They Reveal," echoes a feature in *'Teen*.[11]

Alas, for all the parlor-room fun it can provide, this approach to thinking about doodles isn't wholly satisfying. The problem doesn't lie with Freudianism, but rather with its tenuous application to doodling. It is ultimately impossible to use Freudian concepts to definitively understand subjects without direct, extensive access to the people themselves. And so the analysis of any doodle will inevitably be strictly speculative. (Psychologists often make this point. Back in 1947, the shrinks Charlotte Kamp interviewed for her *New York Times* Magazine piece warned that "a really effective interpretation requires some familiarity with the person involved, so that known mental and emotional factors can be associated with the symbols and patterns that go down on paper.") Ultimately, sad to say, we can glean only limited insight into our presidents' inner lives from their White House scribblings.[12]

The appeal of presidential doodles, then, must be located in realms beyond the purely psychoanalytic. We must look also to the American people's long-standing love-hate relationship with their most powerful officer, the president.

* * * *

Americans have harbored ambivalent feelings about the presidency since the office was created. Having thrown off the British monarchy, the colonists insisted on establishing a republican government in which the people would be sovereign–without any sort of magistrate that might so much as resemble a king. But their first stab at a national system, the ill-starred Articles of Confederation, failed precisely because it did not provide for an executive branch–leaving the country united only by what George Washington called "a rope of sand." To remedy the problem, colonial leaders in 1787 convened the Constitutional Convention, where they drafted a new regime that included a strong presidency.[13]

Ever since, the popular desire for both purposeful leadership and an egalitarian system has created a contradictory attitude toward the presidency. Despite the early hopes for a weak executive, the president–as the head of state as well as the head of government–took on a ceremonial grandeur that could be distressingly king-like. The unanimous choice of George Washington to inaugurate the office in 1789 enhanced its mystique. "Babies were being christened after him as early as 1775," Marcus Cunliffe wrote of Washington, "and while he was still president his countrymen paid to see him in waxwork effigy." Although Washington reassured the country that he had no monarchical pretensions, his stature inevitably invested the office with majesty.[14]

This veneration for the president has remained acute–even in this cynical modern age. The most powerful official in government, the president comes closer than any other individual to embodying the nation itself. Theodore Roosevelt once remarked after a tour of the West that people had come to see him because of their "feeling that the president was their man and symbolized their government . . . they had a proprietary interest in him and wished to see him . . . they hoped he embodied their aspirations and their best thought." The president still serves as a repository for such hopes and desires (and fears and nightmares). With posh inaugurations, a resplendent mansion, his own plane, and even his own theme song, the chief executive enjoys a status unmatched by any of his countrymen. Presidents, not senators, typically adorn our currency, and no chiseled mountain face bears the likenesses of our top Supreme Court justices. For all the power recently ascribed to other government officials, it's still rare to hear a proud parent talk of wanting her child to grow up to be chairman of the Federal Reserve.[15]

Studies have demonstrated that the president is the symbol through which children first comprehend their government, even when they have no clue what he actually does. When a president dies, adults experience symptoms of grief they otherwise exhibit only at the loss of their own family members. Not even a president's aides are immune from the office's shamanistic pull. Nixon's White House Counsel John W. Dean wrote of his mental associations upon considering how to "protect the President" during Watergate: "The President. I felt myself rising instinctively in salute. I thought of aircraft carriers, battles, strong men reverent at the mention of his name, a communications network that flashed each utterance around the world." The president has become, too, the cynosure of Washington journalism, generating more news copy than any other American.[16]

For all the pomp and deference, however, Americans also know that the president is just another man. Public officers, Alexis de Tocqueville wrote, "are perfectly aware that they have gained the right to hold a superior position in relation to others, which they derive from their authority, only on condition of putting themselves on a level with the whole community by their way of life." It was in Tocqueville's day—when the voting public first grew in size—that presidential candidates began casting themselves as simply first among equals. Pioneering the image of president as everyman, Andrew Jackson used campaign literature touting his generosity, his humble origins, his lack of elite schooling, and his distance from Washington power brokers. His rowdy inauguration, at which hordes of drunken admirers stampeded over the White House furniture, affirmed in a perverse way the rough-hewn new president's oneness with the people.[17]

Over time, other customs that separated the president from the people eroded. For most of the nineteenth century, for example, presidential contenders didn't campaign personally. A candidate was a "mute tribune," standing aloof from the mean business of politics while others championed him. Toward the century's end, however, self-styled reformers, troubled by corruption and popular ignorance, sought to curb the political machines. They told citizens to judge office-seekers on their individual merits, not their party affiliations. Personality became more prominent in the presidential discourse. Reporters plied a new form of journalism–the political profile–that gave readers a fuller account of the candidates' backgrounds and human qualities.[18]

Taking office in 1901, Theodore Roosevelt embodied the modern president as personality. Whereas in the 1860s the face of even a famous general such as Ulysses S. Grant was mostly unknown to Washington reporters, TR–with his toothy grin, his trademark pince-nez, and his tightly buttoned suits, reproduced in papers everywhere (thanks to the invention of the Kodak camera as well as better printing technology)–was instantly recognizable: an icon. With his activist view of the office and his native gift for newsmaking, TR magnetically drew attention to the office. His boisterous brood of children, his penchant for outrageous behavior, and his taste for consorting with the fledgling White House press corps–he held forth with reporters while getting his afternoon shave–all turned the presidency into a spigot of news for the new mass-circulation dailies. Much of it was unrelated to policy or politics, such as the 1904 *New York Times* article about his pet parrot, Loretta.[19]

Helped along by new media, TR's successors perpetuated the personalization of the office. Under Warren Harding, a publicity hound, "clothes, tastes, pets, amusements, and habits were always on public parade," wrote Lindsay Rogers, a political scientist of the day, "and an ex-newspaperman was attached to the White House staff to think up ways of 'selling' the president." Calvin Coolidge bantered with reporters at languorous press conferences, belying his reputation for silence, and his radio addresses brought the president's voice into living rooms for the first time. With his fabled "Fireside Chats," Franklin D. Roosevelt used his unmatched gift for conjuring intimacy with the public to endear himself to millions.[20]

Even more than radio, television created a deceptive public sense of personal closeness to the president. If the new medium bolstered his clout, it also reduced his grandeur, making him appear overly familiar and smaller than life. The plainspoken Harry S. Truman, after moving back into a renovated White House, led a team of TV reporters on a tour, stopping abruptly to rattle off a Mozart sonata on an East Room piano. Jackie Kennedy reprised the gimmick some years later, minus the sonata. By the Kennedy years, pundits were discussing whether the front-page newspaper diagrams of Eisenhower's intestines that ran during his illness or the widely seen photos of Kennedy's bare chest at poolside meant that presidents had now forsaken their private lives altogether. (In retrospect, it's striking how much Kennedy managed to keep private.)[21]

Since the 1960s, other factors have further diminished the presidency's mystique, if not its actual power. Vietnam and Watergate dispelled much of the president's heroic aura. The era's skepticism toward authority made doubting, attacking, mocking, and knocking our leaders seem as reflexive as a military salute and as American as the Kentucky Derby. In 1970, George Reedy discerned "the twilight of the presidency." In 1992, *Time*'s headline "The Incredible Shrinking Presidency" morphed from coinage to cliché overnight.[22]

Perhaps more than any of his predecessors, Nixon showed the public that presidents could possess all the ordinary vices of the common man—and some extraordinary ones too. His own machines recorded him cursing, fuming, badmouthing his enemies, and plotting petty acts of revenge. The upshot wasn't just a more cynical view of presidents as flawed and human; it was a redoubled impulse to scour the psyches of elected leaders for signs of irrational (not to say paranoid) Nixonian behavior. This pop psychoanalytic scrutiny wasn't new. It had gained currency in the 1950s when Nixon was vice president, a heartbeat away from the cardiacally challenged Eisenhower. In those early years of the atomic age, the scuttlebutt that Nixon visited a Park Avenue psychoanalyst fed emerging worries about the emotional stability of whoever might have his proverbial finger on the button. Similar fears destroyed confidence in Republican presidential nominee Barry Goldwater in 1964, whose shoot-from-the-hip style and comments about using nuclear weapons in Vietnam–coming just two years after the Cuban Missile Crisis–scared away voters. In 1972, news that George McGovern's vice presidential nominee, Thomas Eagleton, had received electroshock therapy for depression helped force him off the Democratic ticket. Watergate simply confirmed that some link existed between private neuroses and public actions. Americans resolved to look closer the next time.[23]

"Character" fast became the watchword among Washington reporters, tacitly deputized by a wary public to probe the lives of aspirants to high office. Claiming "I will not lie to you"–itself a lie–Jimmy Carter shrewdly rode the character wave into the White House. As public and private converged, new and arbitrary elements of a politician's private life–past drug use, marital infidelity, military service–were suddenly deemed fair game for journalistic scrutiny. This jerry-built conception of character didn't produce more honest leaders, but it did help demolish the wall of propriety that once surrounded the Oval Office. The new standards were applied retroactively, too. After Watergate, biographers dredged up untold tales of Kennedy's womanizing and flocked to the once-disreputable subject of Jefferson's slave-owning.

The repeal of Victorian mores, underway for decades, also proceeded apace; the personal became the political, and vice versa. As First Lady, Betty Ford went public with her breast cancer and then her alcoholism. Carter confessed in *Playboy* to lust in his heart. Ronald Reagan's colon was televised. When Clinton divulged to an MTV audience his preference for briefs over boxers, what was shocking wasn't his candor but that his candor could still rile a few puritans. Sometimes even the president of the United States has to stand naked.

Today we see as many signs of the president's ordinariness as of his eminence. Prosecutors, pundits, kibitzers, and barflies all inveigh that "no one is above the law." Office-seekers vie to shed elitist trappings; Ivy League degrees and Mayflower pedigrees go unmentioned on the permanent campaign, as candidates boast of their common roots and contrive a common touch. Clearing brush, chopping wood, munching pork rinds, tossing the first pitch: the populist style pervades the political sphere.

Political rhetoric has grown more familiar. Reflecting our therapeutic ethos, presidents use "I" and "you" more than they used to and babble to reporters about their feelings as if confiding to a therapist. The presidential family has become a mainstay of campaign-trail theatrics. After his groundbreaking use of autobiography in his 1952 Checkers speech, Nixon won fame–and shame– for trotting out his wife, Pat, and his daughters as verbal and physical props; "George Washington never said how glad 'Martha and I' were for the tributes of the crowd," sneered JFK supporter and historian Arthur M. Schlesinger, Jr., in 1960. A generation later the tactic wasn't even controversial. George Bush, Sr., explained that seeing Michael Dukakis's son on TV in 1988 led him to respond in kind. "We've got a strong family, and we watched that and we said, 'Hey, we've got to unleash the Bush kids.' And so you saw ten grandchildren there, jumping all over the convention." They've been jumping ever since.[24]

Political audiences, as much as political consultants, have contributed to the humanizing of the presidency. A book-buying, *Booknotes*-watching public devours the newly minted genre of "presidential history," whose bestselling works dwell less on policies and ideas than on personal lives: Washington's character, Adams's marriage, Jefferson's slaves, Lincoln's depression, FDR's affairs, Kennedy's illness, Johnson's ego. We seek these glimpses though the Oval Office curtains because they promise to let us reconcile our ambivalent feelings toward the president: in revealing our fascination with his every tic, we pay obeisance to his importance even as we cut him down to size.

Probably the most important factor whetting this appetite for details about the personal lives of presidents has been the transformation of presidential politics into a vast made-for-TV spectacle. With a mammoth apparatus of speechwriters, press officers, pollsters, and image-makers at the president's disposal, any glimpse of his private side now promises a smidgen of authenticity in an otherwise never-ending political drama. Hence, we're tantalized by a chat with the First Lady, a purportedly spontaneous "town hall" meeting, a secret White House tape, a gaffe uttered unwittingly into a live microphone or on a rolling camera, a choke on a pretzel–and, perhaps, a presidential doodle.

Presidential doodles are intriguing, above all, because they provide us with a glimpse of the unscripted president. They're the antithesis of the packaged persona. Made with neither help from speechwriters nor vetting by a focus group, a doodle is the ultimate private act; its meaning may remain opaque even to the doodler himself. As a result, it renders the president human in ways that a staged family outing cannot. And if we can't make conclusive judgments about what a president's drawings reveal about his innermost fears or fantasies, his doodles can still be suggestive and provocative. They're of interest *cumulatively*: side by side, the scores of doodles in this book reveal the range and diversity of the styles and mental habits of the men who have led this country. Collectively they help in a benign and inviting way to demystify the office–to build a bridge between citizen and leader.

The styles of presidents and the copiousness of their output vary widely, and they tell no neat chronological story. Yet over the long term, some evolution in the presidential doodle can be discerned. For the earliest presidents, true doodles are hard to find. The scribbles included herein by George Washington, the John Adamses, and a few others come from boyhood copybooks or diaries or pre-presidential notes. Still, in their elegant or haphazard scrawls–or in Thomas Jefferson's architectural drawings and codes for writing secret letters–we see gratuitous flourishes, absentminded repetitions, and daydreamed designs that exude the kind of unmistakable pointlessness that makes a doodle a doodle.

Full-fledged presidential doodles start to appear in the 1820s and 1830s, with Presidents Jackson, Van Buren, and William Henry Harrison. On the whole, however, the nineteenth-century record is sparse, at least when compared to the doodle-rich twentieth. To what extent our long-ago presidents idly etched is, unfortunately, unknowable because many didn't keep their papers. It's a sad fact for a presidential buff to learn that for most of American history, presidents privately owned their official papers and many collections were lost, destroyed, or scattered among different libraries. The Library of Congress opened its Manuscript Division in 1907 and set about acquiring what remained of many presidents' collections. But even among those that survived, how much had been deemed expendable and discarded along the way is unknown.

That changed in 1939, when FDR decided to donate his papers to the federal government and provided land on his Hyde Park estate for archives to house them—the first presidential library. Roosevelt even sketched plans for the building (and for such details as the lighting fixtures) in doodle-like designs. His friends and associates raised the necessary funds.

Roosevelt's successors followed this model, in which the public owned and the government administered presidential papers, with private financial support. In 1955, Dwight Eisenhower made this formula official by signing the Presidential Libraries Act. But two decades later, Nixon's conduct in office exposed the need for reform. Nixon had not only tried to abscond from the White House with incriminating documents but also deducted a half-million dollars from his tax returns for donating his papers to the government, in order to reduce his tax bill. Believing that access to presidential papers shouldn't hinge on the charity of the president himself, President Carter signed the Presidential Records Act in 1978. The law declared any records documenting the president's constitutional, statutory, or ceremonial duties to be public property—a broad net that has, happily, swept up some classic doodles in its haul. Of course, some presidents have found or created loopholes. George Bush, Sr., exploited the provision that allows presidents to designate papers as "privileged" and keep them private, and his papers that are open to the people contain almost no doodles.

Despite such connivances, presidential doodles have proliferated in the twentieth century. The reasons are many. History became professionalized in modern times, placing new importance on bureaucratic record-keeping. The executive branch exploded in size, creating larger, longer, and more frequent meetings in which a president might find himself with just a pen or pencil to occupy himself. Improvements in photocopying meant more paper lying around. The telephone became an indispensable tool, leaving nervous presidential hands idle.

It makes sense, then, that Herbert Hoover, who never met a pencil and scratch pad he didn't like, was the first prolific presidential doodler. Hoover's doodles are also historic as the first to enter the public realm. In 1929 an autograph collector named Thomas Madigan bought a Hoover drawing that a White House visitor had taken home, and his purchase garnered extensive newspaper coverage. Articles crowed that the published images would allow readers "to analyze and otherwise sound the mental depths of President Hoover's mental makeup and inner personality, just as it is done in the best psychological circles." Eventually, a dressmaker turned Hoover's design into a pattern for children's rompers, one of which Hoover's granddaughter Peggy Ann is said to have worn.[25]

Franklin D. Roosevelt and Harry S. Truman also doodled, but it wasn't until Dwight Eisenhower took office that Hoover faced a challenge for the presidential doodling crown. A Sunday painter who liked to set up his easel in the White House, Eisenhower put his artistic training to work with pencil and paper during innumerable cabinet and National Security Council meetings. Only after his presidency, however, did the Eisenhower Library put fifteen of these drawings on display–a motley selection of nuclear images, weaponry, tables, pencils, and self-portraits (with hair). John F. Kennedy's doodles were similarly put on public view in the year after his death; they also inspired a sculptor to turn them into "Doodles in Dimension," using steel, aluminum, and wood. More recently, presidential doodles have been sold at auction. One of Ronald Reagan's fetched $10,000–pretty good, considering that Picasso's brought only $40,000. Some celebrities, including presidents, now create doodles expressly for sale at charity benefits–although, to return to Ralph Bunche's important insight, a doodle drawn with such purposeful intent may not truly deserve the name.[26]

The commodification of offhand scribblings and similar trivial effects through auctions can strike us as morally dubious. It privatizes what should be public (selling off presidents' wares to the highest bidder) and publicizes what should be private (putting on display personal drawings or artifacts). But in recent times– the postmodern chapter, if you will, in presidential doodling history–the line between public and private has blurred. Reagan's sketches, fittingly, embody this confusion. Reagan doodled deliberately for admirers who wrote to him at the White House. His drawings were designed to promote the impression– a contrived one, but not a false one–of a light-hearted president, youthful in spirit, freely and earnestly dashing off drawings for his fans. Reagan was aware of the PR value of these aggressively cute pictures. The White House even compiled some of them for scrapbooks. With doodles, as with so much else for Reagan, the traditional distinction between the real and the image collapses.[27]

For Reagan, the knowledge that the press and the historical record were looming over his every move presented a political opportunity. For others, it has been an inhibition. After moving into the White House, George W. Bush–wary like his father of public scrutiny–stopped e-mailing his regular cyber-correspondents, fearing that they would be "subject to open records requests." But no president can keep a hermetic bubble around his personal notes, as Bush found out at the

United Nations in September 2005. When nature called during a speech by the leader of Benin, Bush wrote a note to Secretary of State Condoleezza Rice, as if asking permission from his mother or a teacher: "I think I MAY NEED A BATHROOM break? Is this possible?" Reuters photographer Rick Wilking caught the note on film, to the president's chagrin. Like true anti-Freudians, administration flacks discouraged journalists from reading too much into the note or its timing. Yet it's hard not to conclude that the moment Bush chose for his exit may have been influenced, if only unconsciously, by his level of interest in the concerns of the Third World.[28]

Of course, it's perfectly fair to say of notes like Bush's—and of presidential doodles more generally—that they shouldn't be taken too seriously. But it's also important to remind ourselves that they shouldn't be taken too lightly either. Offering glimmers of and glimpses into the private president, doodles constitute small sources of potential understanding to a public that is forever striving to gain insight into its leaders. After all, the meaning of these doodles is in good measure what we make of them—a liberating and democratic realization, and a statement that's equally true of the American presidency itself.

[1] Richard A. Clarke, *Against All Enemies: Inside America's War on Terror* (New York: Free Press, 2003), p. 86.

[2] Herbert S. Parmet, *Eisenhower and the American Crusades* (New York: Macmillan, 1972), p. 273; George B. Kistiakowsky, *A Scientist at the White House: The Private Diary of President Eisenhower's Special Assistant for Science and Technology* (Cambridge, MA: Harvard University Press 1976), p. 149; Peter Edelman, *Searching for America's Heart: RFK and the Renewal of Hope* (Boston: Houghton Mifflin, 2001), p. 27.; *The New York Times,* December 18, 2004, p. 19.

[3] Michael Balter, "From a Modern Human's Brow—or Doodling?" *Science,* January 11, 2002, pp. 247-248; Matthew Battles, "In Praise of Doodling," *The American Scholar,* September 2004, pp. 105-108.

[4] George Pendle, "New Foundlands," *Cabinet,* Summer 2005, pp. 65-68; "Russell Arundel, 75, Dies, Pepsi Official, Sportsman," *Washington Post,* February 3, 1978, C4.

[5] Russell M. Arundel, *Everybody's Pixillated: A Book of Doodles* (Boston: Little, Brown, 1937), p. ix.

6 W. H. Auden, "In Memory of Sigmund Freud," in *Another Time* (New York: Random House, 1940); Arundel, passim.

7 Charlotte Kamp, "Doodles Are 'Self-Portraits,'" *New York Times Magazine*, June 1, 1947, p. 22; "White House Doodles," *Time*, September 6, 1982, p. 80.

8 Norman Uris, *The Doodle Book* (New York: Macmillan, 1970), p. 72.

9 Uris, pp. 21, 9.

10 "Richard Nixon/Frank Gannon Interviews," May 13, 1983, 41:31-45:26. Available at http://www.libs.uga.edu/media/collections/nixon/nixonday5.html. Accessed on January 4, 2006.

11 S. Lynn Chiger, "Discover What Your Doodles Say About You," *Mademoiselle*, July 1994, p. 144; "Doodles & Squiggles: What They Reveal," *Teen*, October 1993, pp. 96-97.

12 Kamp, p. 22.

13 John Rhodehamel, ed., *George Washington: Writings* (New York: Library of America, 1997), p. 515.

14 Marcus Cunliffe, *George Washington: Man and Monument* (Boston: Little, Brown, 1958), p. 15.

15 Bruce Miroff, *Icons of Democracy: American Leaders As Heroes, Aristocrats, Dissenters, and Democrats* (New York: Basic Books, 1993), p. 180.

16 See for example, Fred I. Greenstein, "The Benevolent Leader: Children's Images of Political Authority," *American Political Science Review* (December 1960), pp. 934-943; Greenstein, "More on Children's Images of the President," *Public Opinion Quarterly* (Winter 1961), pp. 648-654; F. Christopher Arterton, "Watergate and Children's Attitudes Toward Political Authority Revisited," *Political Science Quarterly* (Autumn 1975), pp. 477-496; Paul B. Sheatsley and Jacob J. Feldman, "The Assassination of President Kennedy: A Preliminary Report on Public Reactions and Behavior," *Public Opinion Quarterly* (Summer 1964), pp. 189-215; John W. Dean, *Blind Ambition: The White House Years* (New York: Simon & Schuster, 1976), p. 193.

17 Alexis de Tocqueville, *Democracy in America and Two Essays on America*, (New York: Penguin Books, 2003[1835]), trans. Gerald Bevan, p. 237; M. J. Heale, *Presidential Quest: Candidates and Images in American Political Culture, 1787-1852* (New York: Longman, 1982), pp. 51-63.

18 Michael E. McGerr, *The Decline of Popular Politics: The American North, 1865-1928* (New York: Oxford University Press, 1988), p. 174; Charles Ponce de Leon, *Self-Exposure: Human Interest Journalism and the Emergence of Celebrity in America, 1890-1940* (Chapel Hill, NC: University of North Carolina Press, 2002), pp. 172-205.

19 Thomas C. Leonard, *The Power of the Press: The Birth of American Political Reporting* (New York: Oxford University Press, 1986), p. 100; "Pampered Pets of Prominent People," *The New York Times Magazine*, September 18, 1904, p. 4.

20 Lindsay Rogers, "The House Spokesman," *Virginia Quarterly Review,* July 1926, p. 356.

21 Eric Goldman, "Can Public Men Have Private Lives?" *The New York Times Magazine*, June 16, 1963, p. 13 ff.

22 Michael Duffy, "The Incredible Shrinking Presidency," *Time*, June 29, 1992.

23 David Greenberg, *Nixon's Shadow: The History of an Image* (New York: W.W. Norton, 2003), pp. 239-44.

24 Roderick Hart, *Seducing America: How Television Charms the Modern Voter* (New York: Oxford University Press, 1994), pp. 26-32; Arthur M. Schlesinger, Jr., *Kennedy or Nixon: Does It Make Any Difference?* (New York: Macmillan, 1960), p. 12.

25 Unidentified newspaper article, Herbert Hoover Presidential Library, Herbert Hoover Papers, Post-Presidential Subjects File, Doodles Correspondence 1936–1959.

26 *The New York Times*, April 24, 1986, B6.

27 Michael J. Sandel, "Bad Bidding," *The New Republic*, April 13, 1998, p. 10.

28 *The New York Times*, March 16, 2001, A5; *The Washington Post*, September 16, 2005, A29.

Memorial Verses.

By the Nineteenth Epact to find the Day of Easter Limit from the Beginning of March inclusively

The Epacts taken from 47; but two the Greatest take from 77; t'will do

Example

What was Easter Limit Anno 1707

$19|1700|89$
$\frac{100}{17}$

$\frac{17}{11}$
$30|\frac{110}{6}|6$

$\frac{47}{7}$
$\frac{40}{7}$ Remains
which shews to be 9th Day of April

What is Easter Limit for this Present Year 1746

$19|1747|91$
$\frac{5}{10}$

$\frac{18}{11}$
$30|\frac{118}{10}|6$

$\frac{18}{12}$ had $12\frac{6}{7}$ Days
March the 2 met

What will be Easter Limit 1749

$19|1750|$
$\frac{40}{2}$

$\frac{11}{32}$ Epact
$\frac{47}{14}$
Ans. 25 Day of March the Limit

But when the Epact is 28 or 29 it must be Substracted from 77 that so may remain. And the Next following Sunday after the Limit is always Easter Day

Easter Limit & the Dominical Letter being given to find Easter Day

The Letter more by 4 from Limit take What is Left from nearest Seven shall Easter make

Or thus take the Number of 4 given letter more by 4 from the given Limit and the Residue from 4 Nearest greater Sum of Sevens if Left remainder Added to the Limit the or its except above 31 is Easter Day in March or April

Example

What was Easter Day Anno 1707

$19|1700|$
$\frac{100}{17}$

$\frac{17}{11}$
$60|\frac{110}{6}|6$

$\frac{47}{40}$

$1|1707|3$
486
$\frac{4}{7|2137|2}$
$\frac{305}{3}$

5 40 35 40
$\frac{4}{9}$ $\frac{9}{31}$ $\frac{4}{41}$

Ans. Easter Day is 13 Day of

When is Easter Day this present year 1746

$1|1746|2$
$\frac{486}{4}$
$7|21|06|2$
$\frac{012}{5}$

5 29 21 29
$\frac{4}{9}$ $\frac{4}{20}$ $\frac{20}{1}$ $\frac{29}{30}$

Ans. 30 of March

What will be Easter Day Anno 1749

$1|1749|1$
$\frac{437}{4}$
$7|21|06|6$
$\frac{042}{1}$

5 25 21 25
$\frac{4}{5}$ $\frac{5}{20}$ $\frac{20}{1}$ $\frac{1}{26}$

Ans. 26 of March

GEORGE WASHINGTON
1789–1797

IN THIS PAGE from one of George Washington's boyhood copy-books, the Father of Our Country also stakes a claim to being the Father of the Presidential Doodle. His mind wandering, perhaps, while doing his assignments, young Washington meticulously filled in alternate boxes both in the frame at the top of the page and along the line that runs down the middle. Washington's doodling, however, didn't prevent him from mastering his mathematics exercises. He went onto become a successful surveyor–a career in which drawing lines and crunching numbers served him well.

These math exercises show more evidence of Washington's fastidiousness—the self-conscious, genteel flourishes of his capital letters, the ornate loops and swirls of even small words. Even in his youth, Washington strove to become the model of a Virginia gentleman, and he is known for having studied the "Rules of Civility & Decent Behaviour in Company and Conversation," a sixteenth-century etiquette manual. (Examples: "When in Company, put not your Hands on any Part of the Body, not usually Discovered," "Rince not your Mouth in the Presence of Others.") Throughout his life, Washington fussed over his appearance and paid close attention to the impression he made in high society.

Geometrical Problems

Problem 11th

Having a right Line given how to make a Geometrical Square equal to y given Line

The given Line is R I for Draw y Line A B equal to y given Line y per c A C perpendicular y to y of y length of A B and with the same Distance and Placeing one y t of the Dividers in C and B deserbe two Arches at D and where the said Arches cu teach other Draw y Lines C D y B D

Problem 12th

Two right Lines being given how to find a third which shall be proportional unto them

Let the given Lines be A y B y Draw two right Lines making any Angle at Pleasure as the Lines L M and M N making the Angle L M N then take the Line A in your Divider y Set the Length y of from M to E; also take y Line B and Set y length y of from M to F and also from M to H then draw the right Line E H and from the Point G Draw y line F G parallel to E H so shall M G be the third proportional y Required

"So anxious was he to appear neat and correct in his letters," said the Philadelphia doctor and revolutionary Benjamin Rush, that Washington would copy long letters he had already written simply "because there were a few erasures on it."

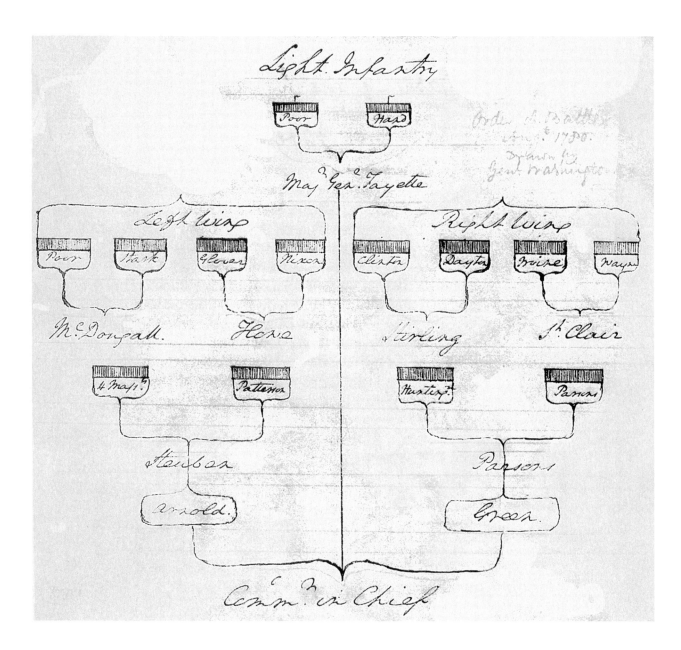

Washington brought his attention to detail to bear when he drew up this order of battle in midsummer 1780. Earlier that summer, 5,000 French soldiers had arrived in Newport to help the Revolutionary Army. Washington had heard about a British plot to lay siege to the arriving French squadron, and he was sending his army to New York to intercept the British before they could carry out their plans.

On July 31, just as Washington was seeing off his last division, Benedict Arnold, one of his generals, arrived. "You are to command the left wing," Washington told him, "the post of honor." It was a generous offer to a man who didn't deserve it; only three months earlier, the Continental Congress had ordered Washington to reprimand Arnold, whom Congress had tried for using army materiel to protect his private property. The left-wing post would have offered Arnold an opportunity to rehabilitate his career and his reputation, and Washington was surprised when Arnold declined it and asked instead for the less prestigious command of West Point. Washington had no way of knowing that Arnold had been negotiating secretly with the British to take control of West Point and turn it over to them in exchange for £20,000. In late September, Arnold's plot was uncovered. He spent the rest of the war fighting for the British.

Now I say that the 3 angles ACD, CDA, and DAC are equal to two right angles. — for it is easy to see $\frac{y}{}$ DCA is a right angle and $\frac{y}{}$ BCE which is equal to CAD added to ECD, which is equal to CDA, make another right angle. — that here the 2 known $\frac{y}{}$ BCE is equal to CAD. Let $\frac{y}{}$ Triangle ECB be moved along to the left had and by the Hypothese CE will fall upon AD and CB upon AC, and of consequence $\frac{y}{}$ 2 angles are equal. — these $\frac{y}{}$ do I know $\frac{y}{}$ $\frac{y}{}$ angle ECD is equal to ADC? see $\frac{y}{}$ Demon. in Euclid. ——

Thence we attempted to demonstrate $\frac{y}{}$ 47th of $\frac{y}{}$ 1st Books. $\frac{y}{}$ $\frac{y}{}$ Square of $\frac{y}{}$ Hypothenuse is equal to the Squares of both the Legs —

JOHN ADAMS
1797–1801

JOHN ADAMS—lawyer, diplomat, philosopher, founding father—served as Washington's vice president before succeeding him as chief executive. Brusque and dour, Adams made political enemies easily. Like Washington, he left no record of presidential doodles, only the geometric problems he solved as a boy. But in his dense, uneven drawings—see his diagram of the Pythagorean theorem at the bottom of the facing page—his rough, cantankerous personality reveals itself just as Washington's smooth, cursive curls reveal his suavity and calm.

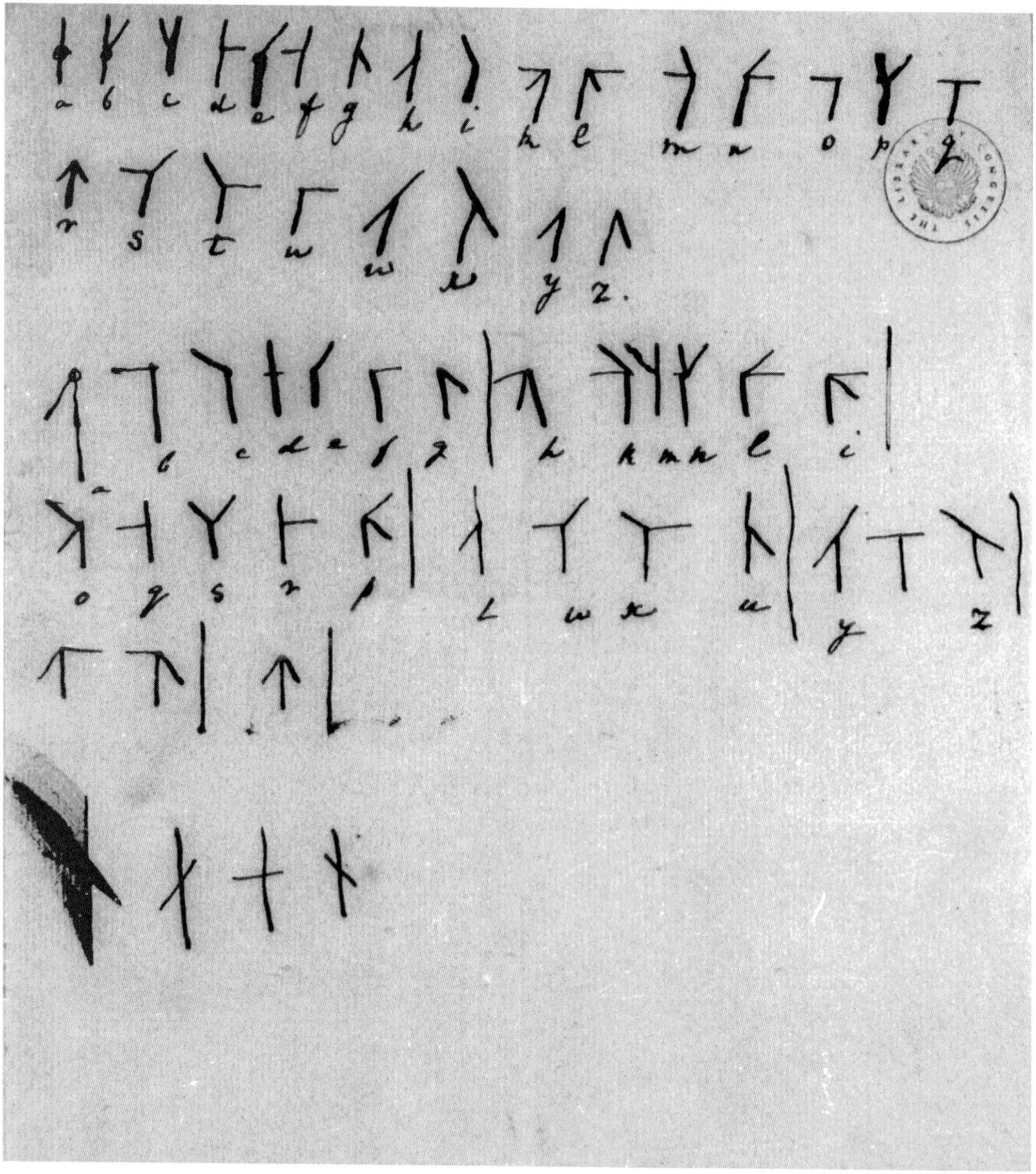

THOMAS JEFFERSON
1801–1809

THOMAS JEFFERSON BEQUEATHED many drawings to posterity. He was constantly making notes on paper, covering pages with mathematical equations and sketches of various sorts. His wide-ranging interests led him into explorations as an architect, an inventor, an agronomist, and perhaps most intriguingly, a cryptographer.

During the Revolutionary War, Jefferson took to inventing codes to keep messages secret from the British. In later years, he kept up the practice to conceal communications from Indian enemies or European postmasters, who routinely opened mail. In the 1790s, he went so far as to invent a complicated device known as a cipher wheel, which generated a new alphabetic code with each use and which could be deciphered only by a recipient with an identical contraption.

This system of chicken-foot symbols was far less ambitious than the cipher wheel, but also more user-friendly, not least because it didn't require Jefferson's correspondent to possess a cipher wheel.

A skilled draftsman and an influential architect, Jefferson designed not only Monticello but every house he ever lived in, at least as an adult. He even set to work on the White House surroundings after becoming president, sprucing up Pennsylvania Avenue with rows of trees.

Long enamored of the pastoral ideal, Jefferson favored openness in all his designs. This 1807 drawing is the plan for a flower garden at Monticello that he called the "Roundabout Walk." He wanted the flowers and winding paths to be not secluded but, as he wrote, exposed to "the workhouse of nature . . . clouds, hail, rain, thunder, all fabricated at our feet." His slaves tended the garden, but Jefferson himself, assisted by his daughters and granddaughters, took great pleasure in planting the flowers in springtime.

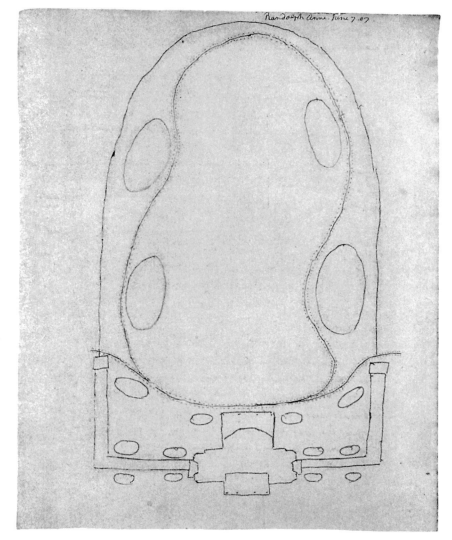

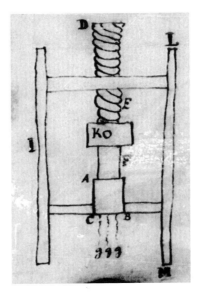

Jefferson was a noted epicure and acquired a taste for Continental cuisine while visiting Europe. During his extended stay between 1784 and 1789, he discovered delicacies including fine French and Italian wines and blancmange, a kind of almond pudding. He became particularly enamored of pasta, especially the kind he tasted in Naples–so much so that he stuck a feather in his inkwell, sketched out a design, and called it a maccaroni [sic]-making machine. Jefferson came to enjoy macaroni and cheese while abroad and served it in the White House in 1802.

You are hereby appointed president of
The Baltimore Shithouse Cleaning
Society.

> By order of the Committee
> Jeremiah Jingle Bolloc
> Acting Secy.

I hope you will accept my old
(i.e. cock). You are worthy of the appoint-
ment and it is worthy of you.

> Yours Intimately,
> J. Jinglebolloc

Hurra for the Shitter
Presidents

> J. J.

JAMES MONROE
1817–1825

THE ONLY "DOODLE" found in James Monroe's papers appears to have been drawn for, not by, the president. Writing to Monroe in the summer of 1825, the author identifies himself as Jeremiah Jinglebolloc. Scholars of the early republic suspect this was not his real name.

The crude drawing, and the note in which it is embedded, serve as a pointed reminder that long before the laments about today's uncivil society, American political discourse could already be said to be going down the toilet.

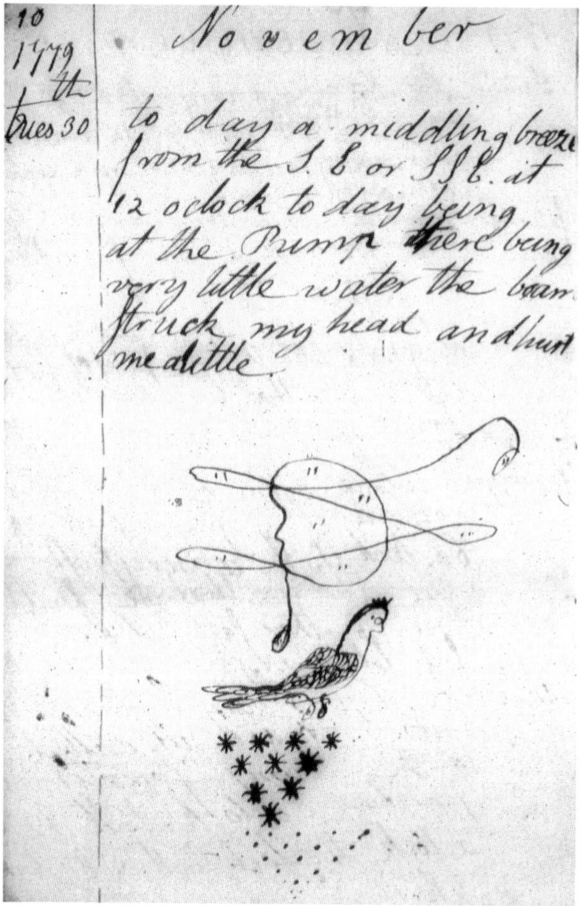

1779

Tues 30

November

To day a middling breeze
from the S.E. or S.S.E. at
12 o'clock to day being
at the Pump, there being
very little water the beam
struck my head and hurt
me a little.

JOHN QUINCY ADAMS
1825–1829

IT WASN'T EASY being the son of the demanding and cranky John Adams. John Quincy Adams–born in 1767, and eight years old when shots were fired at Lexington–grew up with the burden of great expectations. With his father immersed in the affairs of the Revolution and later the birth of the new nation, "Quincy" was lonely and given to self-reproach.

In his letters to his father, who as a diplomat was frequently in Europe, young Quincy sought approval. Avowing his "present determination of growing better," Quincy beseeched his father in one letter to "advise me how to proportion my studies and my play, in writing, and I will keep them by me and endeavor to follow them." As a postscript he added, "Sir, if you will be so good as to favor me with a blank book, I will transcribe the most remarkable occurrences I meet with in my reading, which will serve to fix them upon my mind."

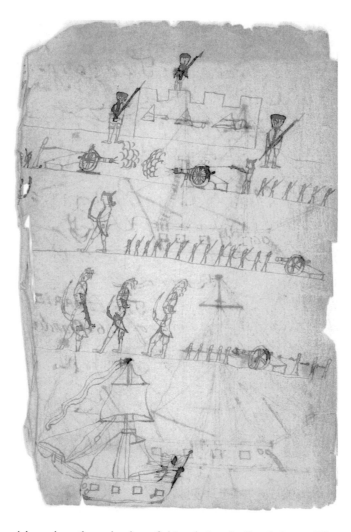

Adams drew these sketches of ships during the Revolutionary War, when the British Navy was anchored in Boston Harbor. Alongside his mother, Abigail Adams, he had watched the burning of Charlestown during the bloody battle of Bunker Hill in June 1775. John Adams, Sr., en route to join the Continental Congress, was cut off from the family during the siege.

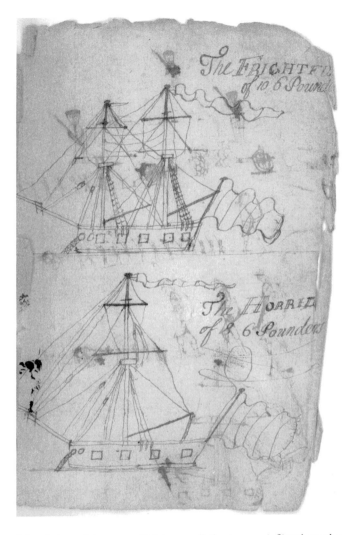

John Quincy Adams would later recall the trauma inflicted on the family: "For the space of twelve months my mother with her infant children dwelt, liable every hour of the day and of the night to be butchered in cold blood, or taken and carried into Boston as hostages, by any foraging or marauding detachment of men." Fantasies of military derring-do naturally found their way into his drawings.

To/The President of the United States
Andrew Jackson Esq
of Tennessee

To

The President

Andrew Jackson Jr

Major Genl Andrew Jackson

Andrew Jackson Jr

ANDREW JACKSON

1829–1837

ANDREW JACKSON SEEMS to be the first president to leave behind full-fledged doodles from his time in office. These drawings–of either a military hat or possibly a tombstone (top), an alligator (middle), and tortoises (?) (bottom)–date from 1833.

Although John Quincy Adams had kept a pet alligator in the East Room of the White House, the animal was more commonly associated with Old Hickory and his martial exploits. An 1828 campaign song, "The Hunters of Kentucky," celebrated Jackson's heroics at the Battle of New Orleans in 1815, noting that in his brigade "Every man was half a horse/And half an alligator."

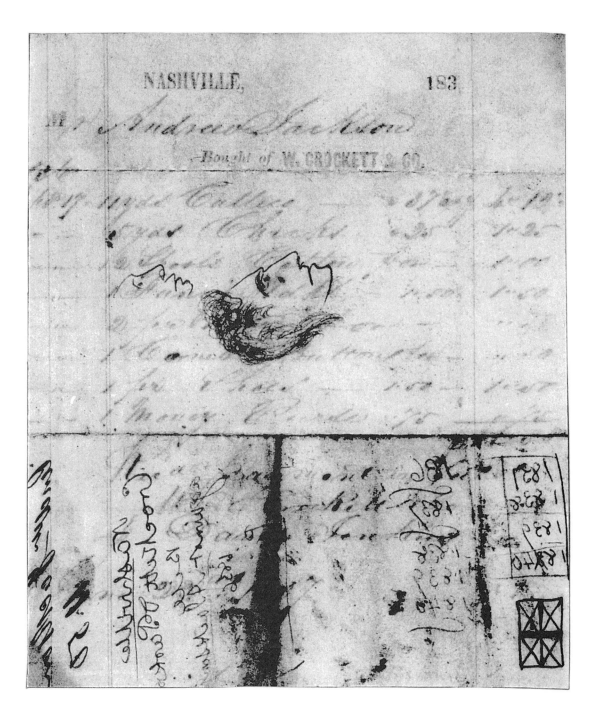

In addition to some *x*'s in squares in the lower-right corner of the page–a favorite image for doodlers in all eras–Jackson also drew faces. He may not have intended the man in profile to represent an actual person, but it does bear some resemblance to the president himself. A similar face appears elsewhere in Jackson's papers, including on several bills and a letter. (Self-portraiture would become a theme in twentieth-century presidential doodling.)

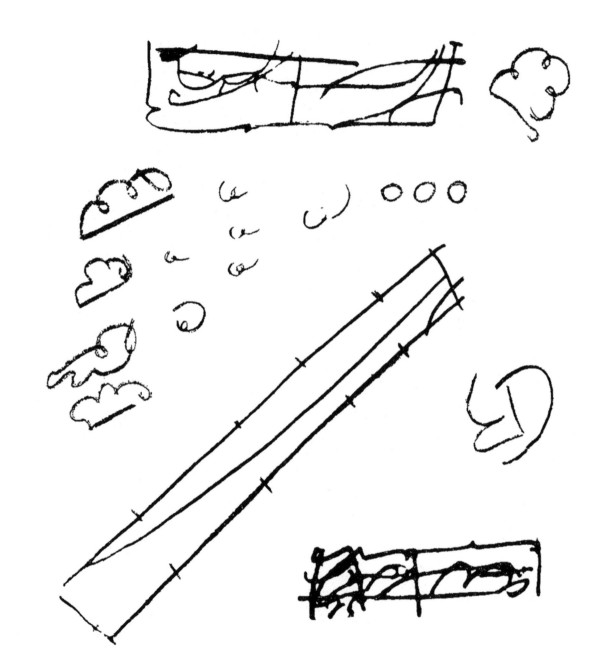

(compilation by Russell M. Arundel)

MARTIN VAN BUREN

1837–1841

WHEN THE ELECTORAL VOTES for president were being counted in 1836, Whig Senator Henry Clay said to Vice President Martin Van Buren, the Democratic nominee: "It is a cloudy day, sir!" Referring to inauguration day, Van Buren replied: "The sun will shine on the 4th of March, sir!" He proved prescient: the sun shone on Van Buren's swearing-in. But clouds–far more menacing than the fluffy ones he doodled here–seemed to be hovering over his presidency, which coincided with a financial depression that led the public to turn him out of office after one term.

"with which he" — strike out "he" & insert "Mr. Adams" —

in the orig⁸

"played the part of the Roman eloquent" — presented - appeared?

those — his ?

Was he in the Senate ?   proposition - proposed ?

Query = "quasi" ?

proposition — "resolution" or
"bill" ?

Mem.
Examine cotemporary authorities for }
the facts of this scene —

"unemiable" — "scribbed" in the original

In several manuscripts, including this set of notes about editing a manuscript, Van Buren doodled a pointed finger. Such pointing fingers were used as editorial marks since at least medieval times; readers of illuminated manuscripts used them to denote insertions and corrections, and Bible readers drew them to call attention to important passages. Called a hand, a bishop's fist, a mutton fist, or a manicule, the icon is a kind of precursor, if you will, of today's computer mouse pointer.

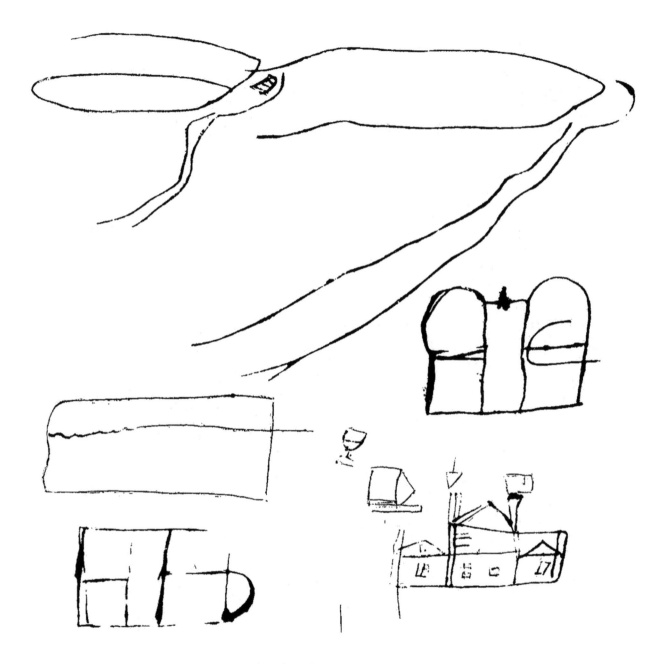

(compilation by Russell M. Arundel)

WILLIAM HENRY HARRISON

1841

WILLIAM HENRY HARRISON may be the only president who has gone down in history as the answer to a trivia question. He served thirty-two days in office before dying of pneumonia, which he caught after delivering his record-breaking two-hour inaugural address in foul weather.

The first president to die in office, Harrison left behind one telling doodle, of a wine glass (at the center of the page). Alcohol played a prominent part in Harrison's presidential career. In the run-up to the 1840 election, a Democratic newspaper dismissed the retired military hero as a senile country bumpkin: "Give him a barrel of hard cider, and settle a pension of $2,000 a year on him," advised one reporter, "and my word for it, he will sit the remainder of his days in his log cabin . . . and study moral philosophy."

It was just what Harrison's party, the Whigs, needed. They were searching for a way to appeal to the masses of new middle-class voters who had made Jackson president and the Democrats the party of "the common man." Seizing on the reporter's remark, the Whigs repackaged their faltering candidate as a man of the people, going so far as to hand out cider in log-cabin-shaped bottles to Harrison supporters on the campaign trail. They played up the imagery in songs mocking Harrison's reputedly vain and aristocratic opponent, Martin Van Buren:

> *Let Van from his coolers of silver drink wine*
> *And lounge on his cushioned settee,*
> *Our man on a buckeye bench can recline,*
> *Content with hard cider is he.*

That image of Van Buren was largely false. Although he could sometimes appear pompous, the Democrat came from humble origins, while Harrison was the classically educated scion of a wealthy Virginia family. As this doodle shows, he was no stranger to wine glasses.

In testimony whereof I have hereunto set my hand and seal, as commissioner appointed by said decree, this   day of   in the year of our Lord one thousand eight hundred and forty two —

43338   [Ac. 9151]

ABRAHAM LINCOLN
1861–1865

GIVEN HIS SOMBER personality, it's not surprising that Abraham Lincoln didn't litter his notes with wild and crazy cartoons. The closest approximations of doodles in his papers are squiggly circles, sometimes with the word "seal" inside. These hand-drawn seals were common in the antebellum period and were often used in lieu of stamps on official documents. This one (bottom right) comes from a legal document Lincoln prepared during his early career as a lawyer.

ULYSSES S. GRANT

1869–1877

AS A YOUNG MAN at West Point, Ulysses S. Grant was a mediocre student. He was, however, an accomplished equestrian. His classmate James Longstreet, who went on to become a Confederate general in the Civil War, described Grant as "the most daring horseman at the academy."

Grant came by his skills at an early age. As a toddler, he enjoyed swinging on the tails of his father's horses. When neighbors warned the child's mother of his dangerous antics, she dismissed their concerns by explaining that "horses seem to understand Ulysses." Ulysses understood them as well; as a teenager, he earned his keep by training horses in his native Ohio. At West Point, during his graduation exercises, Grant jumped his horse so high that the record stood for twenty-five years.

Painting was Grant's other great love at West Point, and he whiled away many an hour with his watercolors. Horses were among his favorite subjects.

10 Author of
Sherman's march to the sea

Rebel Engineer come into Petersburg
after the fall.

Series C

Series D.

Not 3 a Further account of Warren's fight on Whitehall
road.

b On Hundred guns fired over victory. Stopped all
celebration.

Hood 3 Corps Infy — 45000 Stewart
Lee, Cheatham — Nov. 29th & 30th Schofield

d Franklin — See Sherman —
P. 214 Hood's loss buried in field 1752, in
hospital 3800, prisoners 702.
Schofield loss 189 killed — 1033 wounded
1104 Captured and missing. Thomas
organized employees in Ordnance Tower
armed 15th and 16 dec. battle of Nashville

R.

Comment further about
Note S [Rebel] soldiers from east would flock
to his standard — further effusion of blood
and Treasure

Grant's presidency, marked by scandal and the drift of the Republican party into corporate influence, was widely considered a disappointment, especially after his brilliant career as the general who won the Civil War. In like fashion, his presidential doodles are underwhelming compared to the accomplished paintings he made as a cadet. His presidential doodles are unfailingly nondescript: *x*'s, boxes, and other geometric shapes in unimaginative combinations.

Toward the end of his life, Grant began writing his memoirs. He raced to complete the manuscript as he was dying of throat cancer. Mark Twain, who owned a small publishing company, published the memoirs, and both Twain and the Grant family profited greatly when the two volumes became bestsellers.

These pages are taken from a draft of the manuscript. The doodles may be uninspiring, but the memoirs were not. Twain (who had an interest) described them as "the best of any general's since Caesar." Today, they're considered among the finest military memoirs ever written.

RUTHERFORD B. HAYES
1877–1881

O *NLY* *TWO* *MEN* in history have become president after losing the popular vote but then winning the electoral college after the ballot of a single Supreme Court justice ended a drawn-out fight over the vote tally in Florida.

Rutherford B. Hayes was one of them.

The 1876 election, which put Hayes in the White House, was a squeaker. The Democratic candidate, New York Governor Samuel J. Tilden, won the popular majority. But the outcome in the electoral college remained in doubt for months because both sides claimed to have won three Southern states–Florida, Louisiana, and South Carolina. In each state, Tilden initially seemed to be the winner, but the Democrats were accused of fraud and voter intimidation, and Republican-controlled state commissions sought to award the electoral votes to Hayes. To solve the dispute, Congress created a fifteen-member commission that included seven members from each party. The fifteenth member was Supreme Court Justice Joseph Bradley, a Republican generally considered to be fair-minded. But Bradley ultimately joined in a party-line vote that awarded the contested votes–and the presidency– to Hayes. It is thought that to head off any additional challenges, Hayes agreed to pull troops out of the South, thereby ending Reconstruction and letting white "redeemers" establish the Jim Crow system of segregation.

Hayes was a diffident doodler. This woman's face is one of his rare sketches. He drew it in a diary that he titled "Diary of a Deferred Wedding Journey," in which he recounted the details of a weeks-long holiday he took with his wife, Lucy Webb, in 1860. Hayes had married Webb in 1852. She would become the first wife of a president to be officially designated "First Lady."

an affair like this — which swings from side to side of the River by force of the current alone — The boat (whichever way the boat goes) is pulled by means of a windlass up the stream at a small angle — The men employ the Spur —

We returned at 6½ P.M. — The scenery is of the finest — the River is a beautiful clear River — Strange no fish except Catfish — but they are of superior quality and often of great size —

The enemy shows signs of activity in Tennessee again — Our men will have a hard time during the next two or three months, trying to hold their conquests — We will have our day when cold weather and high water return — Not before — About Richmond there is much mystery, but supposed to be favorable —

A meticulous diarist, Hayes kept a daily journal from the age of twelve until his death at seventy in 1893–even as a sitting president and during his Civil War years. Here he illustrates a "flying bridge . . . which swings from side to side of the river by force of the current alone" that his men had to cross at Packs Ferry, West Virginia, in July 1862, when Hayes was a lieutenant colonel.

The Material prosperity
which we now enjoy ~~is without a~~
~~has known no~~ Paral-
lel in our history —
Labor ~~& Capital~~ finds ready & profit-
able employment in
every field of industry
~~Capital finds safe~~
~~investments — and great~~
~~enterprises invite the~~
~~skill~~ ~~The industry & skill of~~
~~our~~ while much
~~of this prosperity is due~~
~~to causes beyond our control~~ —

The prosperity which now
prevails is without a parallel
in our history — Fruitful
Seasons have done much
but they have not done
all — the nation owes a debt
~~of gratitude to my predecessors~~
~~for wise~~ The preservation of the ~~pub~~
The preservation of the public
credit, and the resumption of specie
payments ~~so~~ so successfully
begun by the administration of my
predecessor, has enabled our people
decum the blessing which the season
brought —

JAMES A. GARFIELD
1881

JAMES A. GARFIELD WAS PRESIDENT for only four months when he was shot by a mentally ill man who had sought the position of United States consul in Paris–despite having no qualifications for the job. Garfield languished for two months before dying, during which time Alexander Graham Bell designed a metal detector in an attempt to find and dislodge the bullet. (No one realized that Garfield's metal bed frame was causing the mechanism to malfunction.)

A pack rat and passionate archivist, Garfield often wrote "To be preserved" on the back of letters before filing them away for safekeeping, and in his diary he sometimes recounted time spent "writing and arranging my correspondence." Nonetheless, his archives turned up only a few noteworthy doodles. Most disappointingly, the president, who could simultaneously write in Latin with one hand and Greek with the other, left no example of his dexterity in his files.

This page, covered with scribbles and squiggles, is from the first draft of Garfield's inaugural address. The speech went through at least eight drafts, each containing many deletions, corrections, and revisions. A version of this passage did make it into the final draft, which read:

> The prosperity which now prevails is without a parallel in our history. Fruitful seasons have done much to secure it; but they have not done all. The preservation of the public credit and the resumption of specie payments, so successfully attained by the administration of my predecessors, have enabled our people to secure the blessings which the season brought.

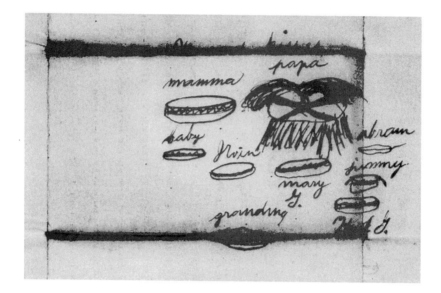

Garfield, who lost his father when he was a year and a half old, filled his letters to his own children with warmth and love. As a congressman, he was often in Washington separated from his family back in Ohio, and he wrote to them eagerly. He routinely addressed his children as "My dear ones," and signed off as "Affectionately your papa." The children wrote to him just as often, with unfailing sweetness and love. They would report on such matters as the words they had missed in their spelling drills and the treats their mother had given them, and they tried to please their father with promises such as "I am going to try to be perfect to morrow."

In this 1875 letter, Garfield drew the puckered mouths of all his family members making kisses: his wife ("mama"); his mother ("grammy"); his daughter, Mary; and his sons, Harry, James, Irvin, Abram, and "baby" Edward.

The issue is now distinctly made between "protection and something that is not protection." To these young men the Republican party, fearlessly accepts the issue and places itself upon the side of the American home & the American working men. ~~You~~ We invite those young men who were too young to share the glory of the struggle for our political unity—to a part in this great conflict for the preservation of our commercial independence.

BENJAMIN HARRISON

1889–1893

LIKE HIS GRANDFATHER William Henry Harrison, Benjamin Harrison has become an anti-celebrity: famous for his obscurity. The novelist Thomas Wolfe had trouble remembering even the basics: "And where was Harrison? Where was Hayes?" wrote Wolfe in his 1934 story "From Death to Mourning." "Which had the whiskers, which had the burnsides; which was which?"

Judged by the standards of history, Harrison made little impact as president. But judged by the standards of presidential doodling, he emerges as something of a star. He left behind some distinctive and appealingly silly cartoons. This figure is wearing what appears to be a Union army uniform and either a cap or a book balanced on his head.

This drawing of a jack-o'-lantern-style face and an ostrich-like bird surely ranks as one of the greatest doodles in presidential history. It suggests a zany, mischievous streak in Harrison, as well as a capacity for conveying a surprising degree of human emotion: shock in the popping eyes, joy in the razor-comb teeth. On the other hand, the absence of hands and feet and the slightly menacing quality of the doodle might also indicate psychosis.

WHITE HOUSE.
WASHINGTON. June 22d
1904

Darling Ethel,

Here goes for the picture letter!

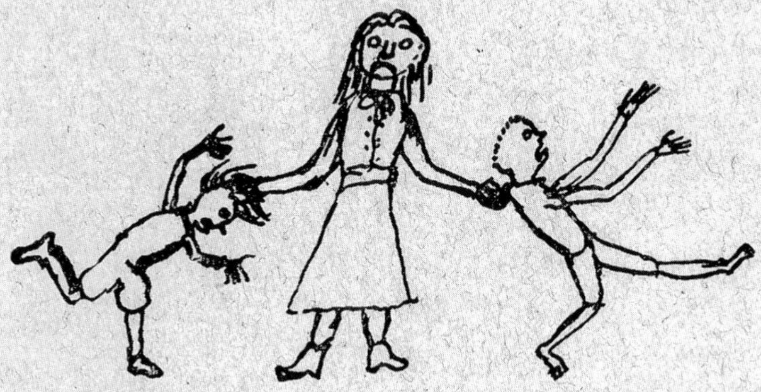

Ethel administers necessary discipline to Archie and Quentin.

THEODORE ROOSEVELT

1901–1909

WHEN WILLIAM MCKINLEY was assassinated in 1901, Theodore Roosevelt, age forty-two, became president. TR remains the youngest chief executive to have served (though John F. Kennedy, who took office at forty-three, is the youngest president ever *elected*). Roosevelt's boisterous brood of six children, to whom he often wrote "picture letters," included Ethel (ten in 1901), Archie (seven, once described by TR as "a most warm-hearted, loving, cunning little goose"), and the runt of the Roosevelt litter, Quentin (four).

Over the years, the boys developed a reputation for mischief. Quentin was known for breaking White House windows playing baseball and for throwing snowballs at Secret Service agents from the mansion roof. He once crashed his wagon into a portrait of First Lady Lucy Webb Hayes. TR was more often amused than angry. "I love all these children and have great fun with them," he wrote, "and I am touched by the way in which they feel I am their special friend, champion, and companion."

A small boy here caught several wildcats. When one was in the trap he would push a box towards it, and it would itself get into it, to hide; and so he would capture it alive. But one, instead of getting into the box, combed the hair of the small boy!

We have a great many hounds in camp; at night they gaze solemnly into the fire.

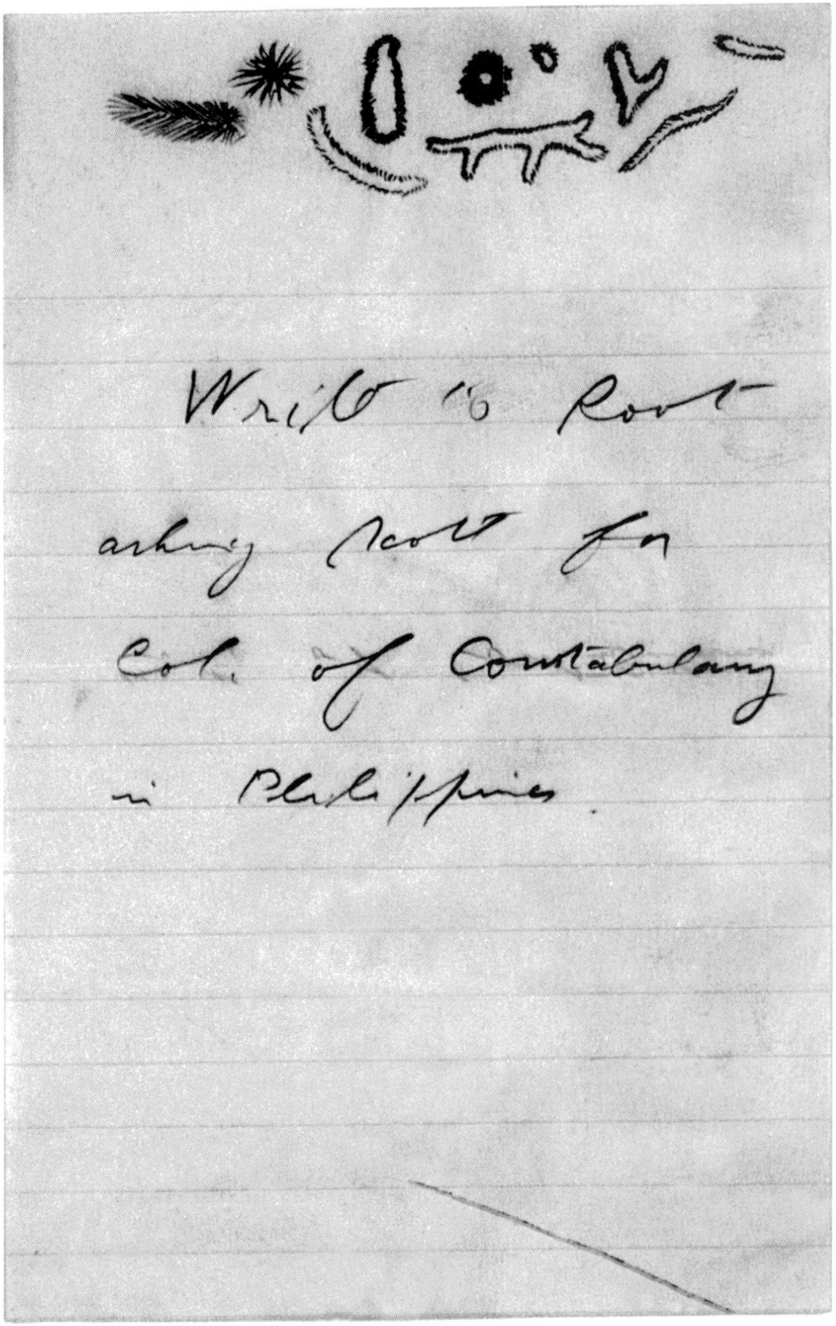

Write to Root asking Scott for Col. of Constabulary in Philippines

Roosevelt loved his audiences, but he also viewed the masses with a condescension that was common to well-born Progressives. He doubted the capacity of American citizens for making subtle distinctions. The public, he once said to his friend Senator Henry Cabot Lodge, "cannot take in an etching. They want something along the lines of a circus poster." TR doodled accordingly, creating artwork fit for a carnival. His unbridled exuberance and slapstick sensibility came through in his drawings for his children (left) as well as in his actual doodles, such as the cat-like figure above.

(compilation by Russell M. Arundel)

WARREN G. HARDING
1921–1923

WARREN G. HARDING IS considered one of the worst presidents in American history. The Teapot Dome scandal–shorthand for a cluster of corruptions and venalities that occurred on his watch–stood as the benchmark for presidential sleaze until Watergate claimed the mantle. But Harding, who died of a heart attack in August 1923, didn't live to see the airing of his administration's dirty laundry–or the exposure of his extramarital affairs, some of which he allegedly conducted in an Oval Office cubicle. During his presidency, in fact, he was seen as a handsome, grand-living embodiment of the Roaring Twenties. His doodles reflect the energetic Art Deco aesthetic: turned sideways they seem to represent the dynamic, grasping, upward thrust of the age, with its skyscrapers, feats of aviation, and conquest of the ether by radio broadcasting.

CALVIN COOLIDGE

1923–1929

WIDELY KNOWN AS "Silent Cal," Coolidge was once approached at a party by a woman who said she'd bet her husband she could get more than two words out of the president that evening. His reply: "You lose." Although his dry wit was often mistaken for dullness, Coolidge could be extremely funny. He would sometimes ring the White House doorbell and then hide behind the curtains when the servants came, or press the buzzer to announce his impending arrival in his office, only to head out the door for a stroll as staffers scurried around to prepare for him.

In 1982, a *Time* magazine graphologist, perhaps unaware that this Coolidge drawing is in fact a compilation of several doodles, discerned "conflicting moods and feeling; the bottom half is precise and calm, but the top half reflects an impatient, unhappy individual." But the assessment was apt. Always withdrawn, Coolidge grew even more so during his years in the Oval Office, in part because of the death of his son Calvin Jr. in 1924. Calvin Jr. had developed a blister playing tennis on the White House lawn. The blister soon became infected—a fatal complication in an age before antibiotics. When he died a week later, the Democratic party was meeting in Madison Square Garden, going through scores of ballots to choose its presidential nominee, but it adjourned for the night in honor of the boy's passing.

(compilation by Russell M. Arundel)

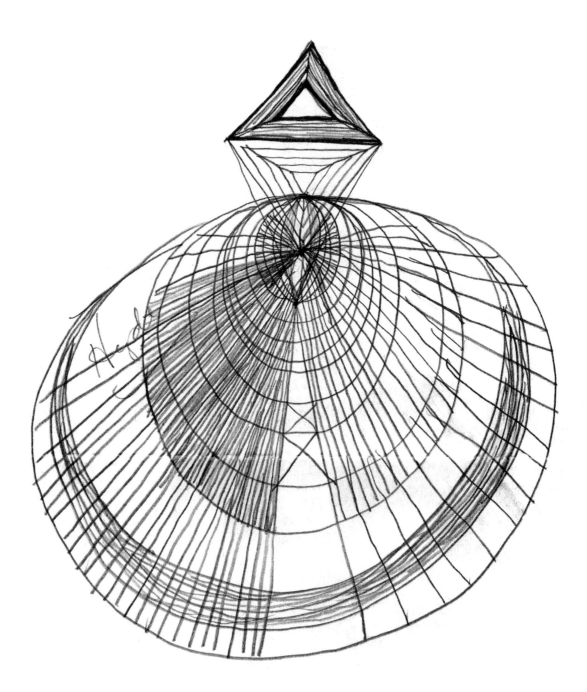

HERBERT HOOVER

1929–1933

MANY PRESIDENTS HAVE enjoyed prior careers as lawyers, generals, or political hacks. Herbert Hoover was an engineer. He brought his engineer's mindset to his presidency and his doodling.

One of the most prolific presidential doodlers, Hoover drew pictures that are consistently geometric, intricate, and clever in the way they link disparate parts into a larger whole. The Technocrat-in-Chief clearly did not lack for imagination: his doodles hint at elaborate and expansive visions. Alas, the same could not be said for his presidency.

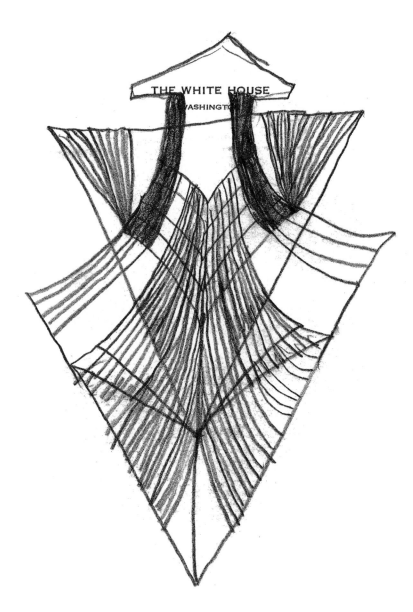

Engineering was more than a job for Hoover; it was his calling. "[It] is a great profession," he once said. "There is the fascination of watching a figment of the imagination emerge through the aid of science to a plan on paper. Then it moves to realization in stone or metal or energy. Then it brings jobs and homes to men. Then it elevates the standards of living and adds to the comforts of life. That is the engineer's high privilege."

Hoover was a master of the abstract doodle. He created dynamic shapes that
suggest diamonds, bow ties, or kites and
achieved three-dimensional effects through
his angling of adjacent lines. But Hoover's
doodles never included any people–
despite his musings here about doing
something "for the American consumer"–
and this blind spot was all too evident in
his slow and ineffective reaction to the
Great Depression. The American public
was hardly blind to this failure, and
Hoover was trounced by Franklin
Roosevelt in the 1932 election.

Despite the rampant anti-Semitism of the 1930s and some ambiguous messages in this doodle, there is no evidence that Hoover blamed the farm foreclosures of the Depression on Jewish bankers.

How many foreclosures –

How many farms without
diversification

How many Bank failures

Mont
North Dak
South Dak

Hoover was the first president recognized in his own day as a skilled doodler. White House visitors sometimes observed him sketching away, and a few reporters made mention of the president's habit. Eventually Hoover's doodling became big news. After he drew the design pictured here, the president tossed it in a wastebasket. A guest retrieved it and got the president to add his autograph. The doodle was then purchased by a collector named Thomas Madigan, who described it as "one of the most unusual presidential autographs I have ever seen." He proceeded to resell it for a substantial sum—"a fair portion of the President's annual salary," according to one source.

The President's Accompaniment to an Interview

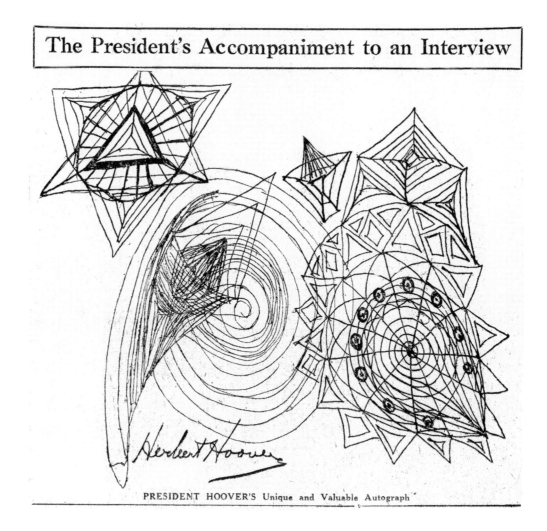

PRESIDENT HOOVER'S Unique and Valuable Autograph

Everybody Does It!

SCRIBBLING BY PRESIDENT IS HELD NORMAL

U. C. Psychologist Studies Free-hand Drawings by Hoover, Scoffs at Character Theory

Pencil line drawings made by President Hoover on a scratch pad when talking over the telephone or being interviewed indicate only that the President is a normal man.

Dr. Walter Brown, head of the psychology department at the University of California, to whom the drawings were submitted for study, scoffed at the theory held by some psychologists that such preoccupied drawings indicate traits of character. He said:

It is the normal thing for a man to do—to occupy himself scribbling with a pencil when talking over the telephone or listening to some one. It would be significant if the President did not do this.

Any one who would attempt to attach any significance to the marks made by President Hoover as indicative of traits of character, would be falsifying.

One visitor, who interviewed the President resurrected a bit of scrap paper on which the President had traced characteristic geometrical drawings while preoccupied.

At the visitor's request, President Hoover affixed his signature and the paper now holds an honored place in the collection of . . . . , New York autograph . . . . It is the most unusual signature ever to come from the White House. Madigan declared.

THERE'S NOTHING extraordinary about a man scribbling—even if he's President. This was the announcement of a University of California psychologist when shown the above "scratchings" on a piece of blank paper by President Hoover while being interviewed. The visitor obtained the scrap of paper and it now holds an important place in the collection of a New York dealer.

Newspapers across the country published the doodle that Madigan bought. Many ran stories containing scholarly analysis of the president's artwork. One expert weighed in for the *Chicago Tribune*: "Generally this man is highly efficient, a man who figures things out and who is at his best tackling difficult tasks." But another expert, speaking to a San Francisco newspaper, dismissed the effort to interpret Hoover's scribbles: "It is the normal thing for a man to do–to occupy himself scribbling with a pencil when talking over the telephone or listening to someone. It would be significant if the President did not do this. Any one who would attempt to attach any significance to the marks made by President Hoover as indicative of traits of character would be falsifying."

Hoover's signature doodle took on a new life as a pattern for children's rompers. Hoover's granddaughter Peggy Ann is said to have worn them on occasion.

Hoover, however, was never thrilled about the publicity his doodling received. In 1936, when Russell M. Arundel, then working as an aide to Rhode Island Senator Jesse Metcalf, sought to reprint a Hoover sketch in *Everybody's Pixillated*, the former president balked. "I do not wish those scrawls published," Hoover replied tersely. "If they have come into anyone's hands, they were persons who had promised not to make public use of them." But several months later Arundel wrote Hoover again, saying that he had inadvertently "failed to withdraw" one of the doodles, which was "scheduled to be printed next week." He added, "I am terribly worried for fear of offending you," and concluded, perhaps as a sweetener: "The election looks sure Republican in R.I." Hoover relented and allowed the doodle to be published.

THE PRESIDENT AS A TEXTILE-DESIGNER! — Miss Irene Colt of the Bureau of Home Economics, U. S. Department of Agriculture, displaying two pairs of Hoover rompers of material fashioned after the geometrical designs which President Hoover absentmindedly jots down on note paper.

(Wide World Photo)

The operations of buying and selling
Commodities for public use or
the provision of services to the
public (except in war or for services
requiring special Confidence such as the post office
or for stimulating the evangoration of service
such as reclamation and waterway improvements)
is socialism pure and simple.
It matters not whether it is disguised
as "nationalization" "government ownership" or
what not.
      Moreover Socialism differs
from Bolshevism — in only one

Although Hoover must be ranked as a great innovator in the annals of
presidential doodling, his modernist designs sometimes stood in sharp
contrast to his retrograde politics. Here, he dashed off one of his smaller
geometric confections in a corner of a page of rants about the danger of
government interference in the economy, which he called "socialism
pure and simple."

Hoover's doodles are like snowflakes: no two are exactly alike. He played with similar techniques and elements over and over, and the drawings at the top of this page suggest variations on a triangular theme. But in the bottom doodle, Hoover abandoned his customary finesse in favor of his Frankenstein mode, creating an architectural monster.

Hoover's post-presidential career, which lasted from 1933 until his death in 1964, was the longest of any president. Asked how he had survived so many years of ostracism during the era of Roosevelt and the New Deal, Hoover stated simply: "I outlived the bastards." Although his reputation was rehabilitated somewhat after World War II, Hoover suffered for many years as a discredited president, a former "Wonder Boy" turned relic of a bygone age.

Living mainly at the Waldorf-Astoria Hotel in New York, his doodling, too, declined precipitously. By the time he drew this particular rendition of his beloved triangles and diamonds, the once-proud utopian designer had clearly lost his touch.

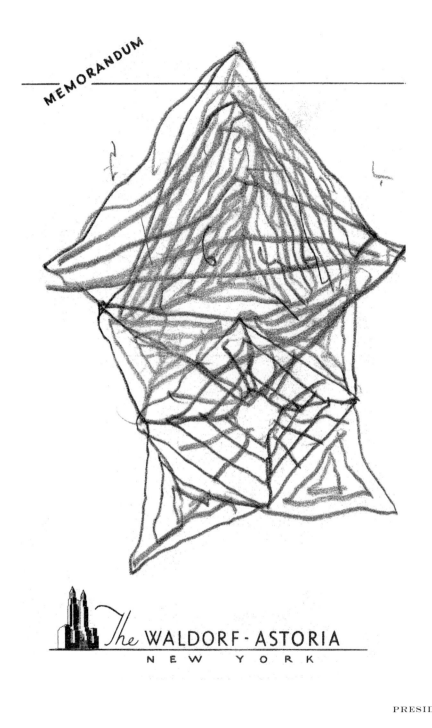

The WALDORF-ASTORIA
NEW YORK

The Cruise Ends.

FRANKLIN D. ROOSEVELT
1933–1945

FRANKLIN D. ROOSEVELT MADE many kinds of drawings during his twelve-plus years as president. Most of them were related to his favorite hobbies: genealogy, stamp collecting, ships, and most of all, fishing.

The president loved going on fishing trips to the Bahamas, the waters off Canada, and elsewhere, usually on the *USS Potomac*. He spent a lot of time planning his trips and often took key advisers with him to discuss politics. In his book *That Man*, Attorney General and future Supreme Court Justice Robert H. Jackson captured the flavor of these voyages in his description of a November 1937 journey.

"The president," Jackson recalled, "got the first fish, a mackerel weighing about twelve pounds, and his pleasure at the catch was marked. [Military aide] Colonel [Edwin] Watson next caught a grouper. His language as he tried to reel the resisting fish in was picaresque and caused great merriment." The next day, Jackson added, the group "enjoyed the president's mackerel for breakfast and Colonel Watson's grouper was served at lunch in a soup made according to the president's recipe. It made a delicious luncheon dish."

This drawing of three fish comes from the final page of a log that FDR kept on a May 1937 excursion to the Gulf of Mexico.

The Wreck

Fascinated by the sea from childhood on, FDR liked to build model ships and collected more than 200 of them in his lifetime. He gained experience with real ships when Woodrow Wilson appointed him Assistant Secretary of the Navy in 1913– a position that attracted him in part because his much older cousin Teddy had held it during William McKinley's first term. (When Franklin was young, he looked up to his cousin, who suggested that Franklin read Alfred Thayer Mahan's *Influence of Sea Power Upon History*. The book, which persuaded TR to develop the American Navy into a world-class force, also made a strong impression on young Franklin, who went on to become a lifelong advocate for the Navy.)

Just as TR parlayed his stint at Navy into a spot on the 1900 Republican presidential ticket as McKinley's running mate, so FDR used his term in the job to become the Democratic vice presidential nominee in 1920, with James Cox of Ohio at the head–an election that Cox and Roosevelt lost. But the setback hardly hurt FDR's career; just twelve years later he was elected president for the first of his four terms.

THE WHITE HOUSE
WASHINGTON
November 16, 1936

MEMORANDUM FOR   THE SECRETARY OF THE INTERIOR

    I still hesitate about "Peg Leg". It
is the best "outside" name I can think of
but it does not connote the double thought
that this is,

    a. Great-Grandfather's Rum come to
        life again, and,

    b. That it is connected with the
        Government.

Will you try again.

    I have little time to much on it but,
attached, is a thought. I think the word
"Colonial", in quotes, is patentable. The
top ship is meant to be a full-rigged sailing
ship of about the year 1800. The lower ship
should represent a very early steamship of
about the 1850 period.

                F. D. R.

Enclosures

PURE
"COLONIAL"
RUM.
Virgin Islands
U.S.A.

Distilled Direct from Pure etc.

This is a rough-draft sketch made by
President Franklin D. Roosevelt himself
of a suggested label for rum manufactured by the
Virgin Islands Company.
with accompanying memorandum initialed by him.

Prohibition was repealed in 1933, early in FDR's first term—a move that helped revive public spirits. The next year, the United States established the Virgin Islands Company (Vico), within the Department of the Interior, to promote economic development in the Virgin Islands, which the U.S. had bought from Denmark in 1917. By 1936, Vico's rum was finding a market and Interior Secretary Harold L. Ickes was tasked with choosing a name and a label for it. He proposed the name Peg Leg Rum to the president. FDR was understandably hesitant. The name they ultimately chose was blander but safer: "Government House." This is FDR's sketch for a label design.

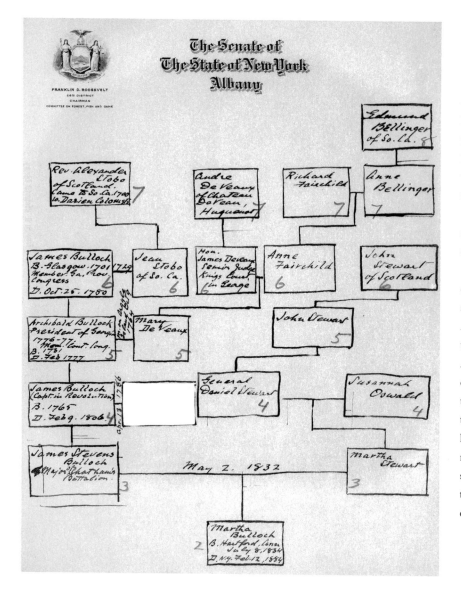

Roosevelt took a strong interest in his own family—so much so that he married his cousin. Among his drawings are a partial family tree and a version of the Roosevelt family coat of arms. The crest was meaningful to FDR; when he was first elected president, in November 1932, he listened to the returns in an oak chair carved with roses based on The crest's design.

As president, Roosevelt played a crucial role in fostering genealogical study in America. The Works Progress Administration—the New Deal organization that put millions of unemployed Americans to work on a range of projects from building libraries to teaching tap dancing—included a division called the Historical Records Survey. The agency hired citizens to compile indexes of last names, vital statistics, cemetery burials, school enrollments, military service, and the like. These surveys have become essential tools for genealogists today.

Franklin D. Roosevelt Library

In addition to model ships, FDR also collected stamps, starting at the age of eight. As president, he traveled with his vast collection, bringing it to Casablanca and Yalta in a large trunk. By the time of his death, he had amassed approximately one million two hundred thousand stamps.

Roosevelt designed stamps for the U.S. Postal Service. In 1934, a citizen activist asked the president to authorize a special stamp for use on Mother's Day mail. Deeply devoted to his own mother, Sara Delano, FDR not only endorsed the idea but created a sketch for the stamp. The Bureau of Engraving and Printing stuck to the president's design, making only small changes, such as adding a bowl of flowers. Postmaster General James A. Farley, a key political adviser of the president's, issued the stamp shortly before Mother's Day that year. FDR later sketched designs for stamps honoring women's suffrage advocate Susan B. Anthony, the original American colony of Roanoke, and other subjects.

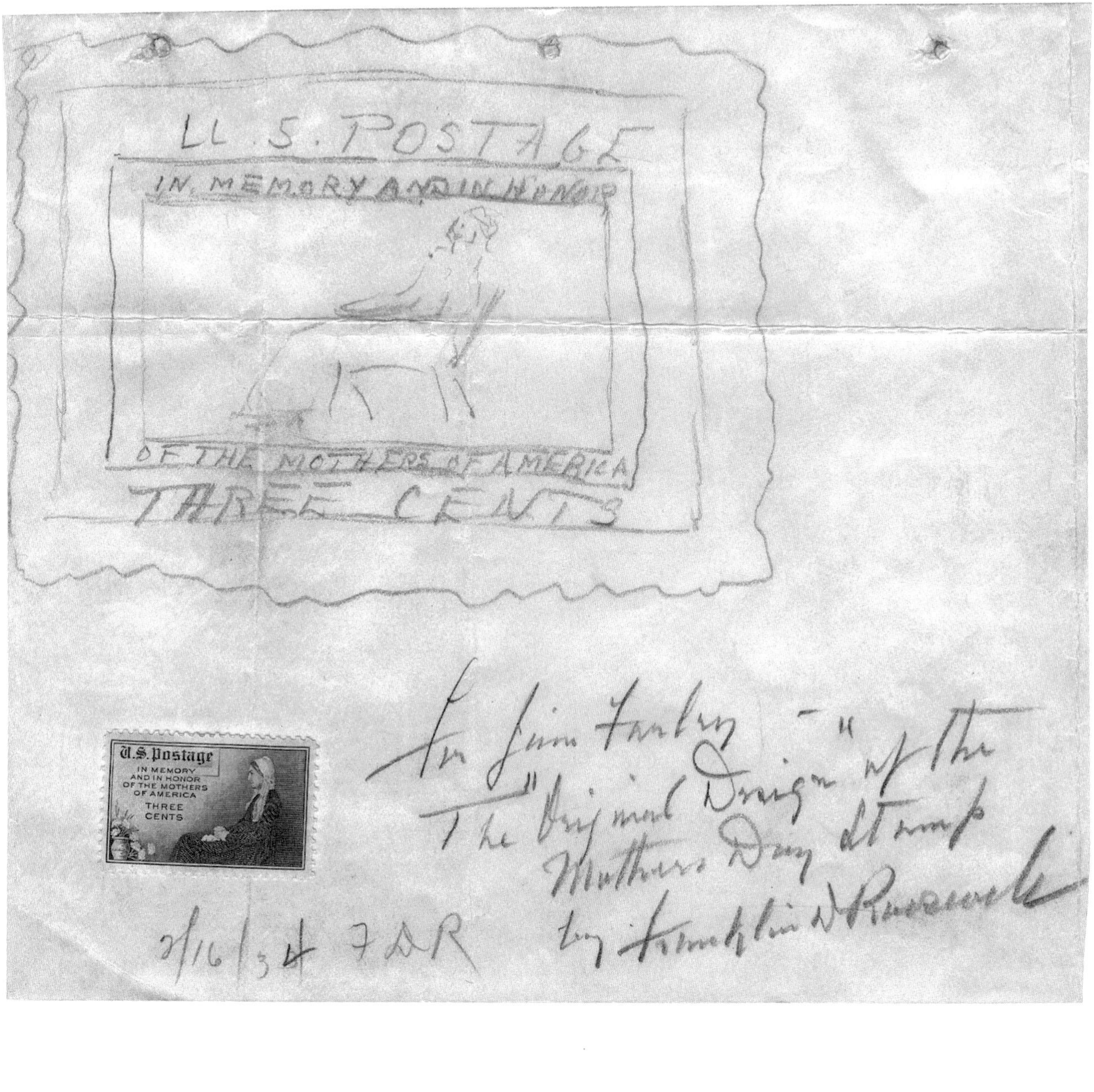

U. S. POSTAGE
IN MEMORY AND IN HONOR
OF THE MOTHERS OF AMERICA
THREE CENTS
U.S. Postage
IN MEMORY AND IN HONOR OF THE MOTHERS OF AMERICA
THREE CENTS
For Jim Farley — "The Original Design" of the Mothers Day Stamp by Franklin D Roosevelt
2/16/34 FDR

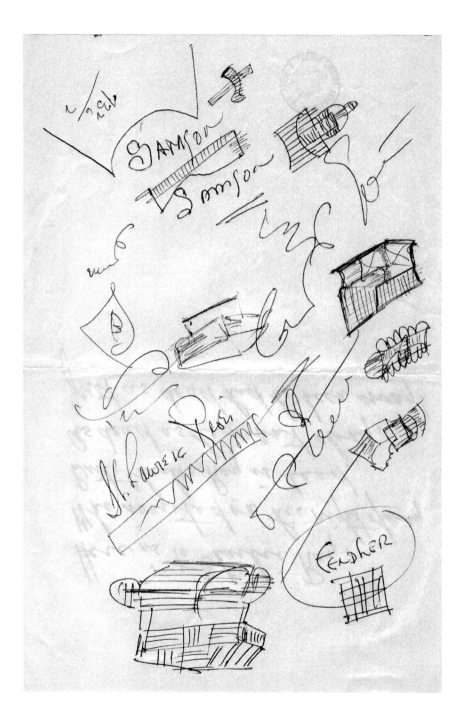

HARRY S. TRUMAN
1945–1953

HARRY S. TRUMAN DIDN'T leave many doodles behind, and those he did were mostly variations on the theme of numbers.

This is one of Truman's more interesting scribbles. He drew it in 1945, the year he became president. He had been vice president for only a few weeks when FDR died, and suddenly found himself tasked with ending World War II. He told one reporter that "I felt like the moon, the stars and all the planets had fallen on me." Certainly, this chaotic doodle suggests that Truman was indeed feeling a bit overwhelmed.

Note the stick figure's hat. From 1920 to 1922, Truman and a friend ran a haberdashery business in Kansas City. They were driven out of business by the onset of the Depression.

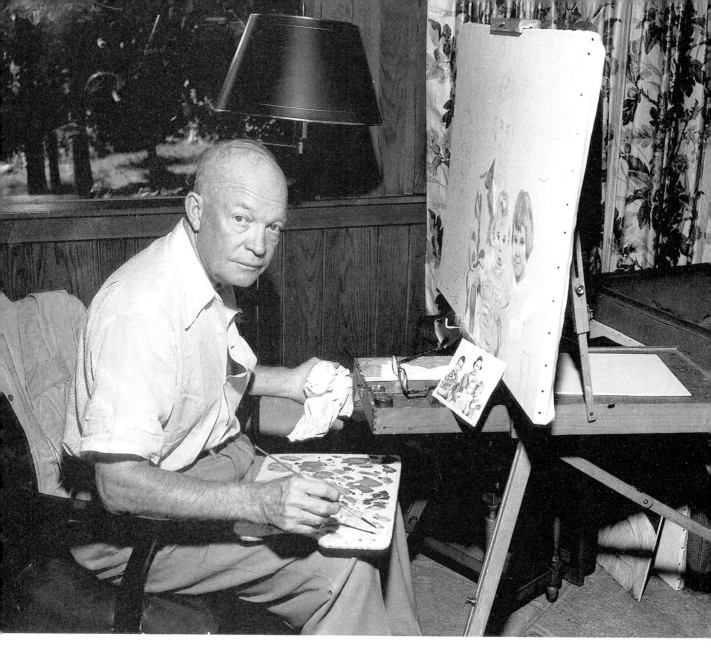

DWIGHT D. EISENHOWER

1953–1961

DWIGHT D. EISENHOWER WAS a devoted and fairly skilled painter. As president, he set up his easel twice a week in the White House (sometimes with the TV going) and turned out landscapes and portraits at a prodigious rate. Painting rivaled his other famous pastime for his affection. "I've often thought," he wrote, "what a wonderful thing it would be to install a compact painting outfit in a golf cart."

Eisenhower's choice of a subject in this painting is telling: George Washington must have been an important role model for the general-turned-president. Where Washington had led the American colonies to victory in the Revolution before assuming the presidency as a man of peace, so Eisenhower, having led the Allies to victory in World War II, ran for president in 1952 on a pledge to end the Korean War. And although Ike was a staunch Republican, he cultivated a political image reminiscent of Washington's—that of a public servant committed to the common good rather than partisan ends.

The Washington portrait also reflects Eisenhower's level of artistic skill: he was reasonably proficient at rendering likenesses but not terribly original (this one is copied from Gilbert Stewart's famous study). Eisenhower reproduced images from postcards, photographs, and even greeting cards. He also used matted prints of his own paintings to adorn his Christmas notes, though claimed he did so with great reluctance. He said he painted simply to relax, never imagining he was composing anything of worth. He wrote to his friend Joyce Hall, the head of the Hallmark Company, which printed his Christmas cards, "As you know, I always hesitate to inflict my 'art' on my friends and members of my staff, but Hallmark makes such a beautiful package job that I am, and I hope others are, distracted into the belief that the whole thing is a superior product."

Ike showed the same uneasiness about displaying his work later in life. In 1967, New York's Gallery of Modern Art (now defunct) hosted an exhibition of his works. Attending the show, the former president remarked that he wished he had burned many of the paintings.

Painted by
Hon Nelson A Rockefeller
of New York
Special Assistant to the President

In the 1950s, a craze for paint-by-number kits, which allowed any-one to produced landscape or portrait just by filling in the right shapes with the designated colors, was sweeping the nation. It also came to the White House, thanks to appointments secretary Thomas Edwin Stephens. (Thomas Edwin Stephens should not be confused with Thomas *Edgar* Stephens, the artist who in 1950 first got Eisenhower hooked on his painting hobby. As fate would have it, Thomas Edgar happened to be a neighbor of Thomas Edwin; they became friends returning each other's mail.)

In 1954, Thomas Edwin Stephens wanted to put on an art display in the West Wing, so he gave paint-by-number kits to cabinet secretaries, administration officials, and other luminaries who paid call on the president. Many of these visitors, presuming that Eisenhower himself wanted them to execute the paintings, returned the finished products to Stephens, who happily installed them as an exhibit in a West Wing hallway. Among the featured works were a dog by Henry Cabot Lodge, a mission church by Nelson Rockefeller, and a Swiss village by FBI Director J. Edgar Hoover. Not shown here, but also exhibited, were works by Attorney General Herbert Brownell, congresswoman and playwright Clare Boothe Luce, and singer Ethel Merman.

Some of Eisenhower's own paintings may have been, in a sense, paint-by-number works. In 1964, Ray Seide, a professional illustrator, claimed that as an army private he had the job of projecting images onto a canvas and tracing their outlines in charcoal, creating shapes that Eisenhower would then fill in with paint.

Given these artistic inclinations, it's not surprising that Eisenhower was a prolific doodler, rivaling Hoover in output. But just as he favored portraits and landscapes in his painting, Ike preferred real objects to abstract designs in his doodling. One of his favorite subjects was himself–often rendered younger and with hair.

Eisenhower's preference for representational art was more controversial than it might seem. He lived in an age of heated artistic controversy: traditionalist critics decried avant-garde movements such as abstract expressionism–Jackson Pollock's paintings were dismissed by one purported connoisseur as mere "childish doodles"–while the art community dismissed such critics as philistines. The conservative president cast his lot with the old-school critics.

In 1959, art and politics collided when an exhibition of American art headed for Moscow was reported to contain a number of avant-garde works, including some by Pollock. The House Un-American Activities Committee investigated. Always the moderate, Eisenhower rejected calls from some on the right that the exhibition be scuttled and redone. Still, he tried to convey his displeasure with the modernist paintings. "We are not too certain exactly what art is," the president said with his characteristically tangled syntax, "but we know what we like, and what America likes–whatever America likes is after all some of the things that ought to be shown."

We recommend, further, that the Federal government encourage the establishment of a corporation by the railroads, as outlined above, and that stand-by legislation be prepared and for the moment kept confidential which would authorize the Federal government to make financial assistance available to the corporation in the event of demonstrated need. (This recommendation was not made by the Cabinet Committee on Transport Policy and Organization.)

With respect to the possible need for direct emergency financial assistance to the railroads, the group has determined that government presently has no authority nor funds for this purpose. Section 302 of the Defense Production Act runs only to loans for the repair or replacement of damaged properties.

Accordingly, we recommend that plans, including a draft of appropriate legislation, be prepared for acquiring the authority and funds by which direct emergency financial aid could be extended by the Federal government in the field of transportation, but that these plans be held entirely confidential until such time (which, hopefully, will not come) when they might be needed. (This was not a recommendation of the Cabinet Committee on Transport Policy and Organization.)

Merger and Consolidation Restrictions

The law as it now stands permits mergers and consolidations of common carriers where the Interstate Commerce Commission finds such mergers and consolidations to be consistent with the public interest. Where the Commission has made such a finding, the anti-trust laws do not apply.

We conclude, therefore, that existing law does not unduly interfere with the opportunity to merge and consolidate, and that no legislative change is necessary.

Government Transportation Activities

Transportation interests frequently find it difficult to get more than partial answers to questions which they pose to Federal transportation agencies. A more effective means of discharging the government's transportation responsibilities and of being able to indicate its interest seems, therefore, not only desirable but necessary. Regulatory agencies in the field, Interstate Commerce Commission, Civil Aeronautics Board, Federal Maritime Board, now operate in a manner so wholly independent of one another that no consistent pattern of Federal regulation is achieved. At the very least, effective liaison among these agencies should be established.

In the Executive Branch there is also widespread sharing of transportation responsibility. While there are three large transportation agencies--the Civil Aeronautics Administration, the Maritime Administra-

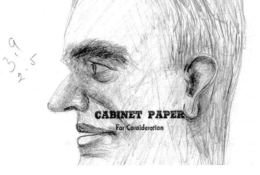

CABINET PAPER

For Consideration

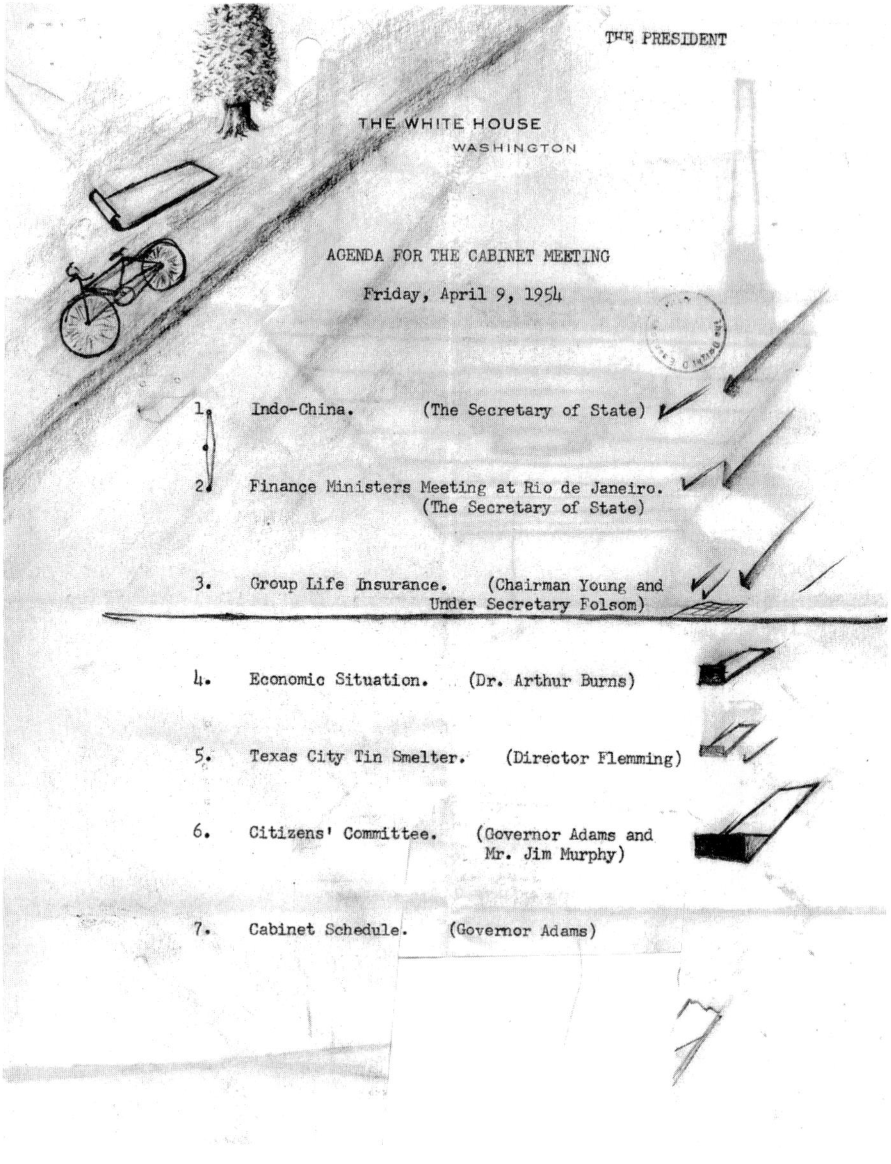

THE PRESIDENT

THE WHITE HOUSE
WASHINGTON

AGENDA FOR THE CABINET MEETING

Friday, April 9, 1954

1. Indo-China.   (The Secretary of State)

2. Finance Ministers Meeting at Rio de Janeiro.
                      (The Secretary of State)

3. Group Life Insurance.   (Chairman Young and
                             Under Secretary Folsom)

4. Economic Situation.   (Dr. Arthur Burns)

5. Texas City Tin Smelter.   (Director Flemming)

6. Citizens' Committee.   (Governor Adams and
                            Mr. Jim Murphy)

7. Cabinet Schedule.   (Governor Adams)

Sometimes Eisenhower's drawings sprung from the idle marks he made on an agenda. Here, a check mark became a sled, which was soon paired against a riderless bicycle racing down a one-tree hill.

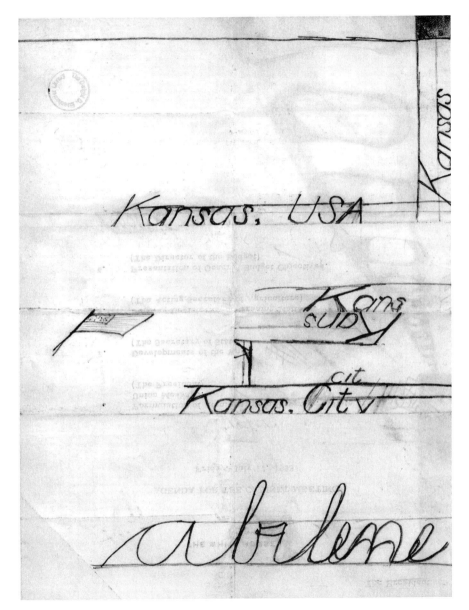

Raised in Abilene, Kansas, Eisenhower often wrote out the name of his hometown and home state. For someone so uninterested in modern art, some of Eisenhower's verbal riffs display a surprising resemblance to the work of his contemporary Saul Steinberg, the innovative *New Yorker* cartoonist (and fellow Hallmark card artist) whose drawings for the magazine are now considered works of art.

LEGISLATIVE LEADERSHIP CONFERENCE

MONDAY, JUNE 28, 1954 --- 8:30 AM

1. Symington Amendment to the Extension of Trade
   Agreements Act   (Secretary Dulles)   *(Guatemala)*

2. Report on Status of Legislation in Senate Finance
   Committee (Senator Millikin)

3. Senate Report (Senator Knowland)

4. House Report (Speaker Martin)

Guatemala

Internal Security

More than any president, Ike doodled on agendas, memos, and other official documents. Their contents afford a glimpse of what was being discussed as the president sketched. This June 28, 1954 memo didn't list the crisis in Guatemala as an agenda item, but Eisenhower did: the day before, CIA-backed forces had deposed the democratically elected leftist government of Jacobo Arbenz in favor of a regime that was more pro-American (or at least pro-United Fruit Company). With Guatemala clearly on his mind, the president sketched himself as a trim, buff young man with big gunboats backing him up—a strong leader restoring order to the strife-torn Latin American nation.

AGENDA
CONGRESSIONAL LEADERSHIP MEETING
Monday, April 26, 1954

1. Senate Report. (By Senator Knowland)

2. House Report. (By Congressman Halleck)

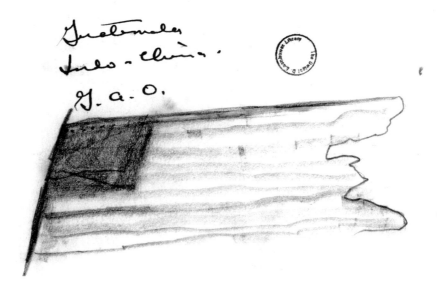

Another Guatemala crisis doodle, from a few months earlier, shows
a battered American flag, seemingly improvised after Ike first drew a
series of horizontal lines with the thick side of his pencil tip. Did he
harbor deep-seated worries that in an age of Cold War militarism
the American Dream was in distress?

Some of Eisenhower's other doodles also have a decidedly Atomic Age feel, incorporating warheads, fallout shelters, and other iconography of the Cold War. The nuclear threat hovers in this memo over issues such as civil rights legislation and veterans' housing—and even lead and zinc legislation.

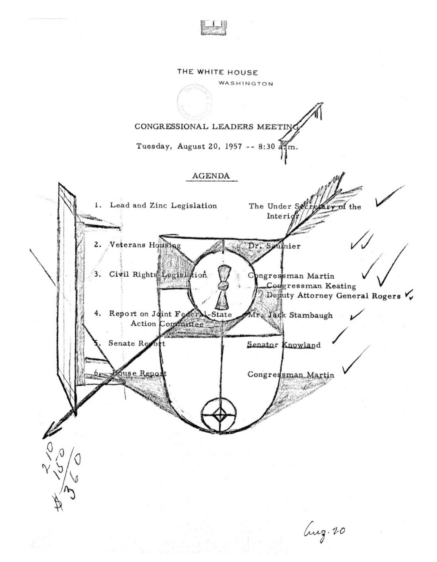

THE WHITE HOUSE
WASHINGTON

CONGRESSIONAL LEADERS MEETING

Tuesday, August 20, 1957 -- 8:30 a.m.

AGENDA

1. Lead and Zinc Legislation   The Under Secretary of the Interior

2. Veterans Housing   Dr. Saulnier

3. Civil Rights Legislation   Congressman Martin
    Congressman Keating
    Deputy Attorney General Rogers

4. Report on Joint Federal-State Action Committee   Mr. Jack Stambaugh

5. Senate Report   Senator Knowland

6. House Report   Congressman Martin

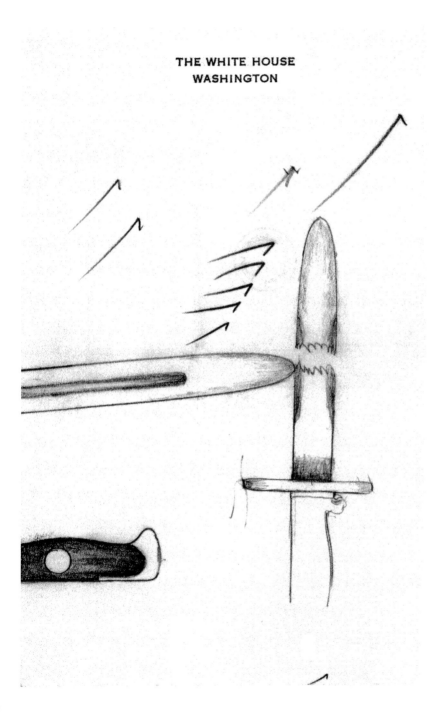

THE WHITE HOUSE
WASHINGTON

A lifelong military man, Eisenhower filled his drawings with pictures of not just nukes but also swords, knives, and weapons of all kinds—with some of his thrusting blades carrying phallic overtones that only the most resolute anti-Freudian could ignore. Eisenhower used art-school tricks such as drawing with the thick edge of the pencil, creating depth and dimension through shadows, and interrupting and resuming a single object with a jagged break—a motif that appears here and in several other Ike doodles.

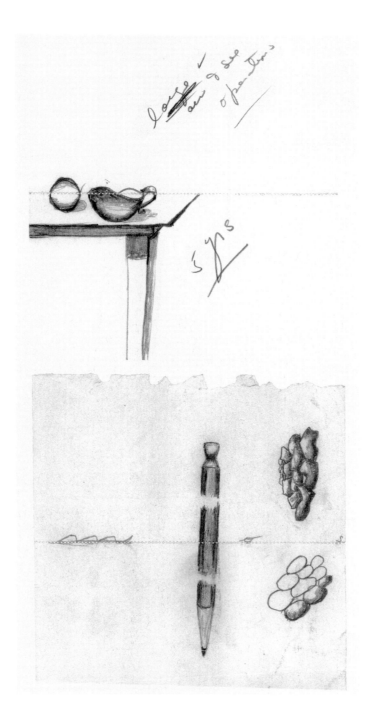

If we define "major" as over 10 minutes,
usually with text, and usually with radio
or radio and television.

8 months May 1, 1957 to Dec. 31, 1957	- 9
12 months - 1958	-27
Total 20 months	36
Jan. 1, 1959 to May 22, 1959	11
Total 25 month period	47

Ike's interests in portraiture and weaponry came together in this sketch drawn in May 1957. The person bears a strong resemblance to Sherman Adams, Eisenhower's chief of staff and most trusted aide. Adams was in fact scheduled to attend the meeting at which Ike probably made this doodle. Sixteen months later, Adams was forced from office for accepting a fur coat and other gifts from a favor-seeking businessman, but it's possible that Ike was already losing patience with his long-standing aide-de-camp at the time of this sketch.

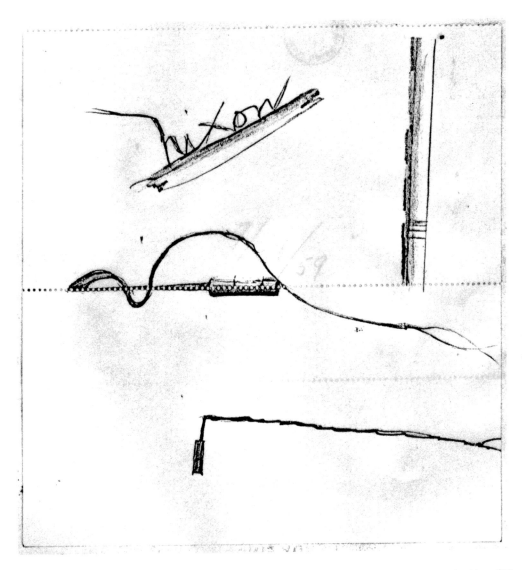

Gentle and avuncular on the surface, Eisenhower could be scathing when he wished. Although in public he usually supported his vice president, Richard Nixon, the two men never became friends during their eight years of service together, and Nixon resented being excluded from Ike's inner circle. During the 1960 presidential campaign, when Nixon was running as the Republican nominee, a reporter asked Eisenhower to name a major idea of Nixon's adopted by the administration. "If you give me a week, I might think of one," he replied. Nixon explained to reporters that the president was probably being "facetious." This image of a whip juxtaposed with Nixon's name, drawn in July 1959, suggests that tensions might have run a bit deeper than Nixon was willing to acknowledge.

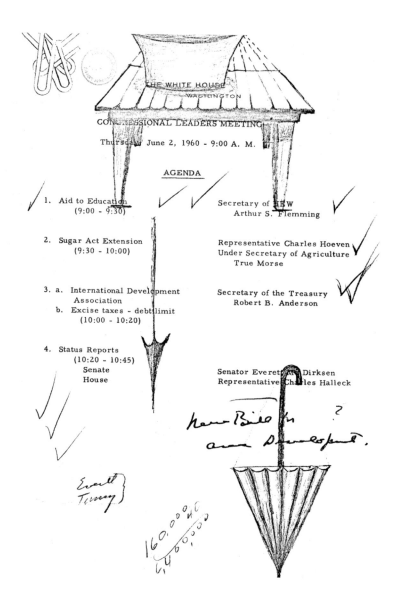

Like the popular images of the 1950s–and like the popular image of Eisenhower himself–Ike's doodles exude sturdiness and solidity. He drew tangible, concrete things: tables, helmets, bowls. But in his sketches, even the most quotidian objects sometimes take on a vaguely menacing tone, such as these plunging, spear-like umbrellas.

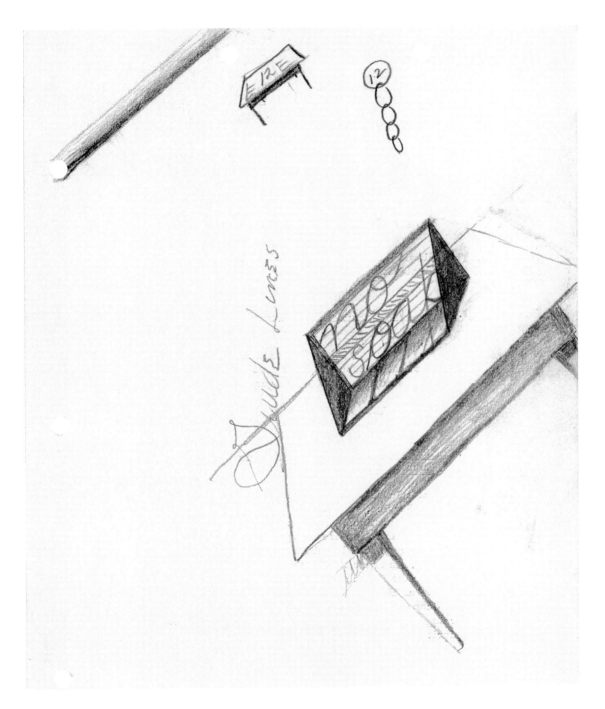

A relic of its time, this FBI document reveals the all-too-common attitude among government and law-enforcement officials in the 1950s that the leaders of the Civil Rights movement were no more justified in their cause or virtuous in their methods than their segregationist enemies. Whoever composed this memo crudely equated the "anti-segregation forces" fighting for racial equality with white supremacist groups such as the White Citizens Councils and the Klan. Making matters worse, the author also made no distinction between the moderate NAACP and extremist groups on the left.

Although Eisenhower drew himself on the segregationist side of the debate here, his actual record was mixed. He sent federal troops to Arkansas in 1957, for example, to protect the black schoolchildren who were integrating Little Rock High School—a move that aligned him with the Communist Party, the "Muslim Cult of Islam," and other groups fighting for civil rights. But on the whole, Ike's initiatives on behalf of black equality were timid. As the Civil Rights movement gained strength during his presidency, he did little to eradicate the Jim Crow system that ruled the South. "I don't believe you can change the hearts of men with laws or decisions," he said in reaction to the 1954 Supreme Court ruling *Brown v. Board of Education* that decreed segregated public schools to be unconstitutional. The end of legal segregation would not come until the presidencies of John F. Kennedy and Lyndon Johnson.

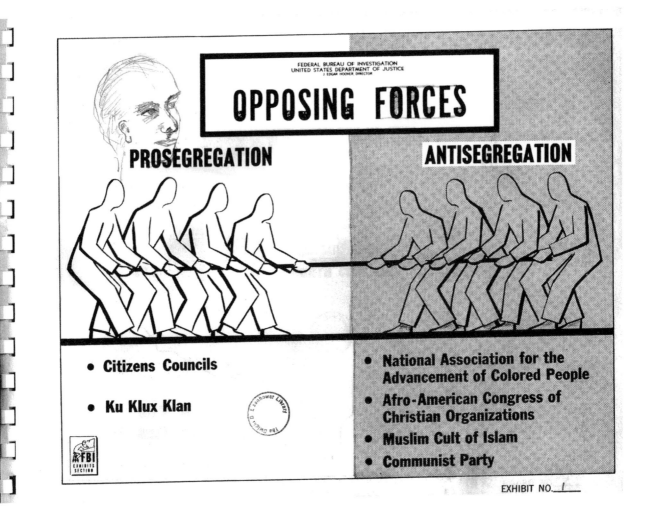

THE WHITE HOUSE
WASHINGTON

JOHN F. KENNEDY

1961–1963

JOHN F. KENNEDY BECAME president at forty-three, the youngest man ever elected. Despite fourteen years in the House and Senate, he had a slender record of legislative achievement. He still had a lot to learn about politics—especially since he took office during the hottest years of the Cold War.

The fight with the Soviet Union for global supremacy dominated Kennedy's presidency. In 1961, JFK launched the disastrous invasion of Cuba's Bay of Pigs, which was supposed to overthrow the newly installed Communist leader, Fidel Castro, and Nikita Khrushchev erected the Berlin Wall, dividing the great German city. The next year saw the Cuban Missile Crisis. Failure was not an option: if diplomacy failed, America could be decimated in a nuclear war.

Cold War references riddle Kennedy's doodles—mainly in the form of words. Where Hoover's doodles are abstract and geometric and Eisenhower's concrete and representational, Kennedy's are heavily textual—reflecting his verbal, cerebral nature. He often repeats a word or phrase several times and sets each one in its own individual box, as if to contain his nervous energy. In a doodle he made during a January 18, 1962, phone conversation with David Ormsby-Gore, the British ambassador, the word Kennedy writes is "awkward." One subject of his discussions with Ormsby-Gore (and with Carl Kaysen, the national security aide whose name JFK has also scrawled) was the disposition of British Guyana, which had recently elected a Marxist premier—an awkward situation, to be sure, as JFK and Khrushchev competed for the allegiance of Third World countries.

Beneath his outward calm and self-confidence, Kennedy could be high-strung. He fidgeted in meetings. "He radiated a contained energy, electric in its intensity," wrote Arthur M. Schlesinger Jr. "Occasionally it would break out, especially during long and wandering meetings. His fingers gave the clue to his impatience. They would suddenly be in constant action, drumming the table, tapping his teeth, slashing impatient pencil lines on a pad. Jabbing the air to underscore a point."

In some doodles, Kennedy wrote one or two or three words over and over, in a tense, almost obsessive repetition—as if he were trying to work through whatever anxious situation was confronting him at the moment. Although one should engage in presidential mind reading with the utmost trepidation, it seems safe to say that in this doodle JFK was concerned about Vietnam. That he encased the word in domino-like rectangles, one tumbling into the next as if spilling across the page, was more likely a felicitous accident than a deliberate visual pun on "domino theory," a phrase that had been in circulation since the 1950s.

The same motif of boxes—frequently filled in with the names of Cold War hot spots—appears in many of Kennedy's notes. Sometimes he draws a chain of boxes, one overlapping with the next, their intersections resembling a row of crosses in a cemetery. In this doodle, Kennedy is focused on the Middle East. The early 1960s witnessed political turmoil in the Arab world. A 1961 coup d'etat brought a Baathist regime into power in Syria; in 1963, the same would happen in Iraq.

Given the number of bizarre conspiracy theories still swirling around Kennedy's assassination, the doodle below—with "9-11" written repeatedly and the word "conspiracy" underlined—is chilling at first glance. On closer inspection, the inversion of the numbers to "11-9" elsewhere on the page and the list of congressmen's names at the top suggest that the numbers refer not to a date but to the possible outcomes of a committee vote.

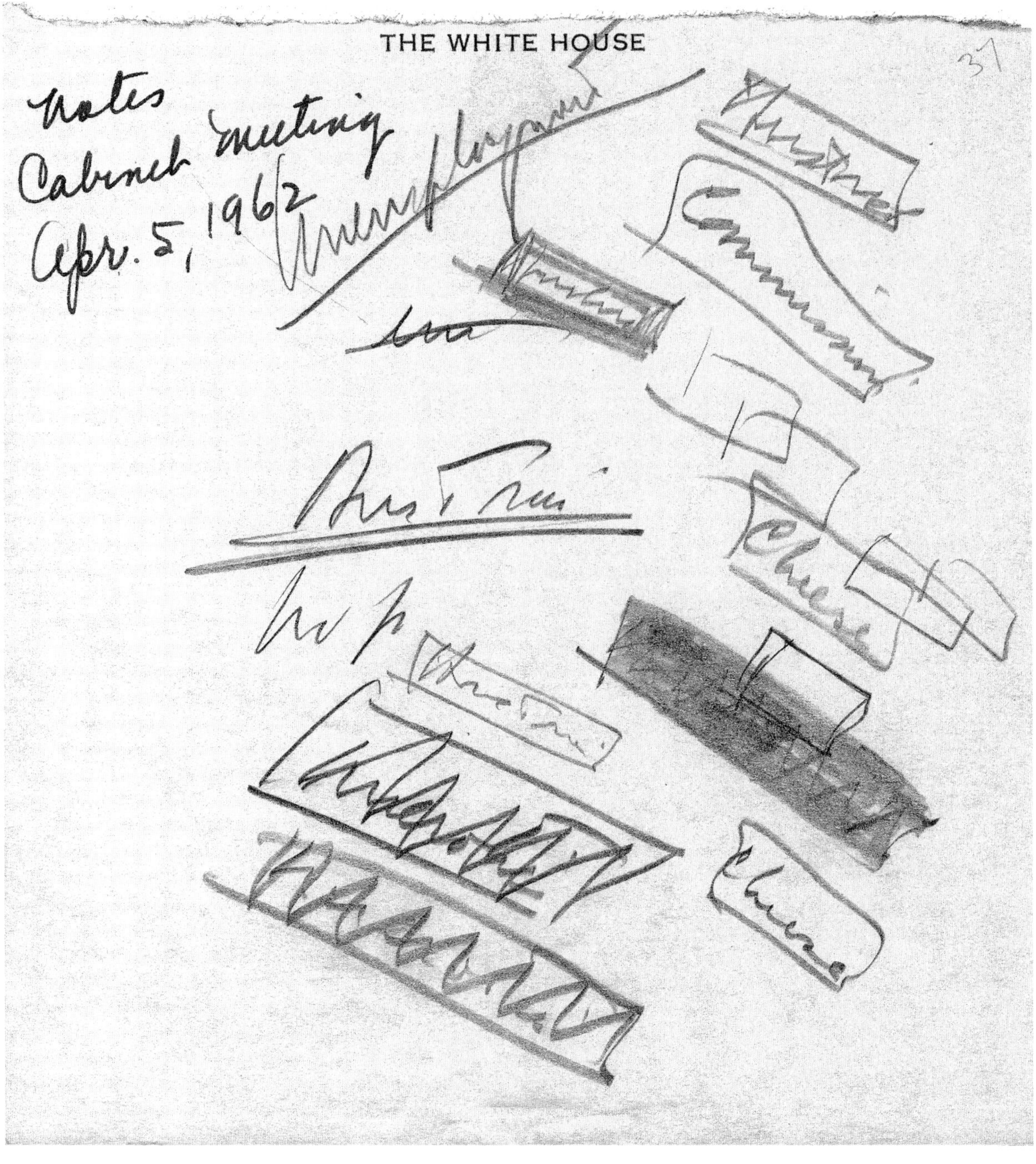

Notes
Cabinet meeting
Apr. 5, 1962

Although foreign policy was Kennedy's main interest, at least at the start of his presidency, his doodles occasionally drift elsewhere. During this April 5, 1962 meeting, Kennedy was apparently thinking not only about communism but also about cheese.

THE WHITE HOUSE

I don't understand all this

Kennedy was known for his "grace under pressure"–a phrase Ernest Hemingway coined and JFK liked. Whether at his live televised press conferences (which he was the first president to hold) or at gatherings of the Executive Committee that met during the Cuban Missile Crisis, Kennedy usually maintained his poise and his ability to think clearly. But the calm sometimes cloaked his uncertainty–an uncertainty the young president may have disclosed in his doodles, as in this where he confesses not to understand the problem at hand, and in the following one, where one can imagine him giving voice to fantasies of escape.

Escape

two
Buchanan

Kennedy resorted to a somewhat strange yet intriguing metaphor in contemplating a showdown with his frequent antagonist Harry F. Byrd of Virginia, a conservative Democrat and segregationist who had served in the U.S. Senate since 1933 and whose seniority gave him substantial power. The two often were at odds over civil rights.

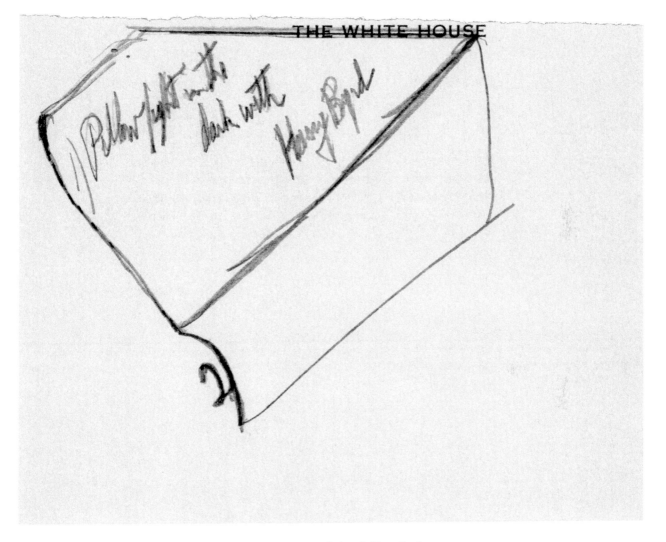

THE WHITE HOUSE

Pillowfight in the dark with Harry Byrd

Some of Kennedy's doodles reveal his wit and whimsy. Here, after compulsively drawing rectangular boxes striped with horizontal lines, he playfully turns those rectangles into two very different images: a musical staff with a treble clef at the left and a modified American flag.

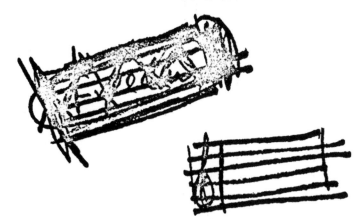

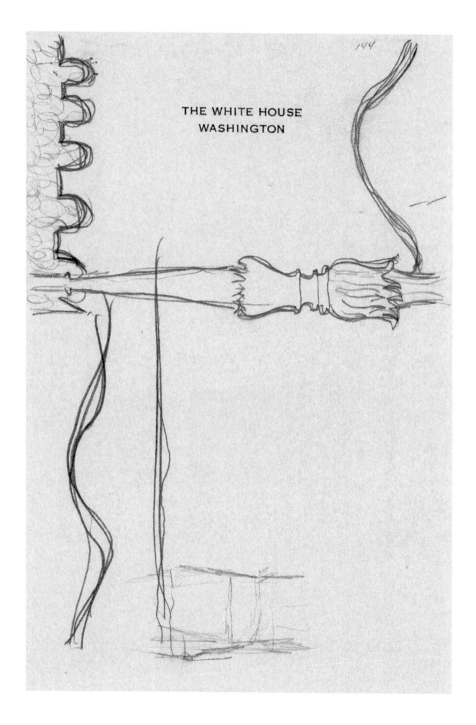

THE WHITE HOUSE
WASHINGTON

Kennedy has been viewed as both a brave Cold War leader and a rascal, an inspiration and a rake. Likewise his doodles are open to vastly different interpretations. The image below might be a torch of freedom being passed to a new generation. Or it might be the ornate pillar of a canopy bed.

Apart from his words and boxes, the image that recurs most often in Kennedy's doodles is the sailboat. In many instances, such as this drawing, he sketched his own sloop, the *Victura*. Built in 1932, entirely of wood, the 26-foot boat was a gift to JFK from his parents on his fifteenth birthday. He raced it as a young man, and it was on this boat that he taught Jackie how to sail.

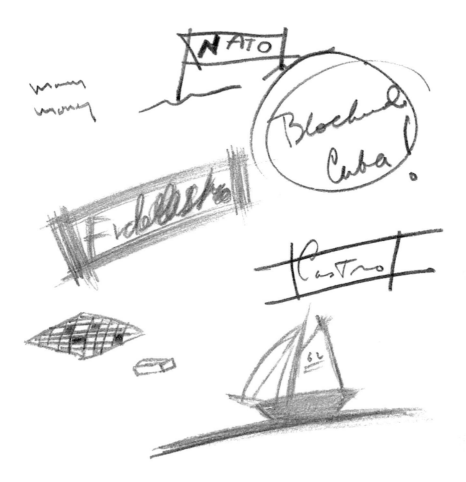

Kennedy drew this doodle during the height of the Cuban Missile Crisis in 1962. "Blockade Cuba!" he reminded himself, much as he might have reminded himself on a slower day at the office to pick up the dry cleaning. During the crisis, Kennedy used Navy ships to blockade the island nation to keep out Soviet missiles. The *Victura*, however, played no role in the quarantine.

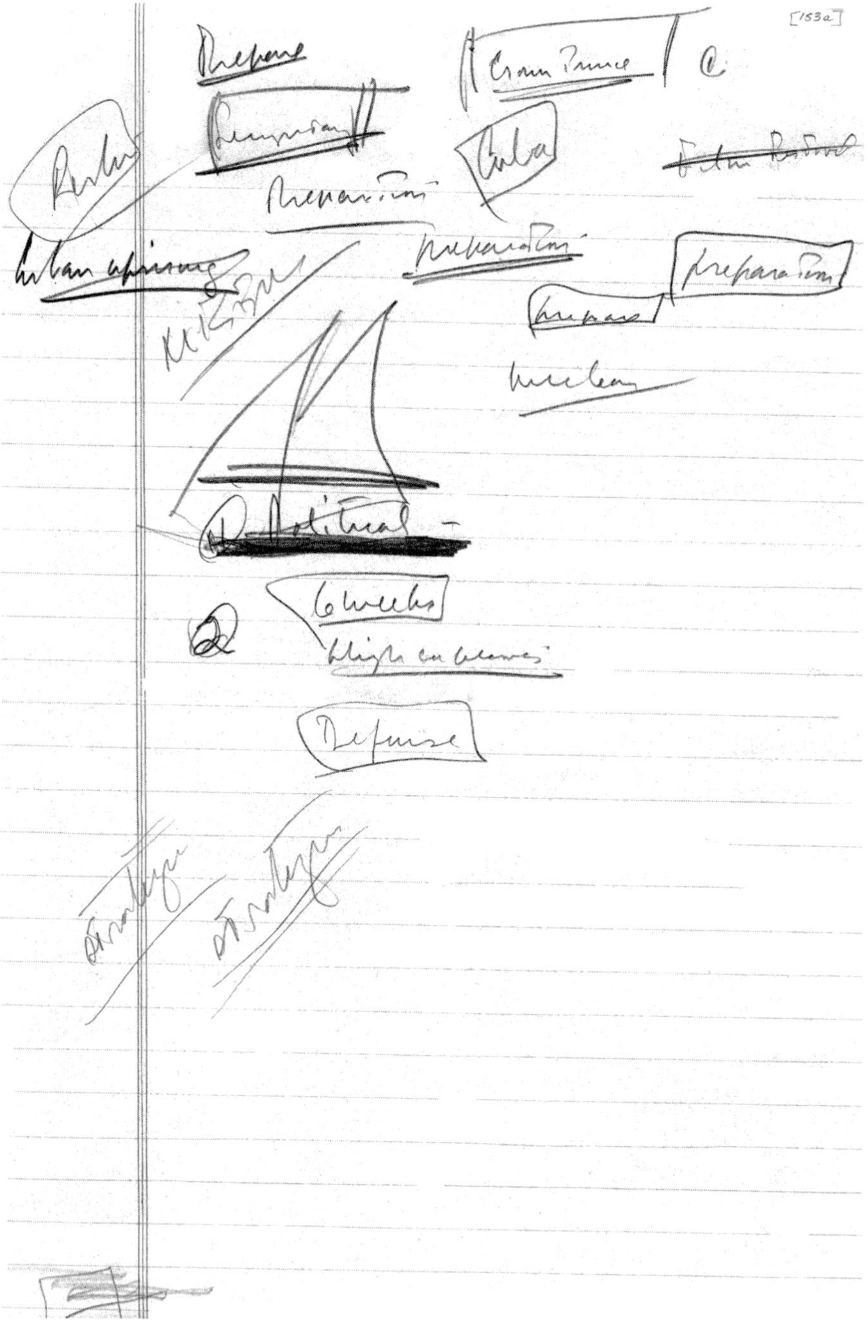

Prepare

Crown Prince ©

Preparation

Preparation

Preparation

Prepare

nuclear

Political

6 weeks

Defuse

Kennedy was never happier than when he was by the ocean. "I really don't know why it is that all of us are so committed to the sea, except I think it is because in addition to the fact that the sea changes and the light changes, and ships change, it is because we all came from the sea," he said at a 1962 dinner celebrating the America's Cup, the international yacht race. "And it is an interesting biological fact that all of us have, in our veins, the exact same percentage of salt in our blood that exists in the ocean, and therefore, we have salt in our blood, in our sweat, in our tears. We are tied to the ocean. And when we go back to the sea, whether it is to sail or to watch it, we are going back from whence we came."

THE RICE HOTEL

"Houston's Welcome to the World"

Kennedy probably sketched this, his freest and most elegant doodle, the night before he was murdered. The stationery in from Houston's historic Rice Hotel, where the president dined and attended a meeting before spending his last night in Ft. Worth. Like the photographs of Kennedy sailing off Cape Cod, this drawing lets one imagine the late president at peace as he pictured himself free on the Atlantic waters.

THE WHITE HOUSE

LYNDON B. JOHNSON
1963–1969

BOTH EISENHOWER AND Kennedy had secretaries who saved their drawings, but Lyndon B. Johnson's White House was probably the most dedicated to doodle collecting. After each meeting, a staff member would round up whatever notes were left in the room, even if they had been balled or ripped up.

Every scrap on which LBJ scribbled was to be preserved. According to the journalist David Halberstam, Johnson was partly motivated by his respect for history and partly by his own grandiosity. "On board the presidential jet," Halberstam wrote, "he often doodled as he spoke with reporters, and if he left to talk with someone else and noted a reporter moving to pick up a scrap of presidential doodle, he did not find it beneath himself to walk back and snatch it away." Over the course of his presidency, Johnson's staff accumulated a substantial file of doodles by not only the president but also by other administration officials and visitors.

It's not always clear which doodles were drawn by LBJ and which by others, although many of the president's have a distinctively aggressive and manic quality, along with a child-like primitivity. The doodle on the opposite page is one of Johnson's finest, with a devilish cat-like animal, a three-headed character in a dress, and a third figure obliterated by violent scrawls.

THE WHITE HOUSE

Although many of Johnson's doodles reflected his explosive personality, others showed a different side of his character, which was coolly measured and systematic. The checkerboard pattern (left) recalls George Washington's meticulous lines, and the grid (below) shows a similar taste for orderly, predictable rhythms. Despite his overflowing, outsized personality, LBJ could summon tremendous discipline when he wanted to pass a bill—or advance his career.

In this doodle, LBJ again shows his strange predilection for drawing figures with three faces. The drawing also reveals his habit of building his doodles around the words "The White House" on his official stationery. On the following pages, Johnson plays on that theme in a variety of ways, turning the name of his residence into a flag, a pagoda, a prison, and other forms.

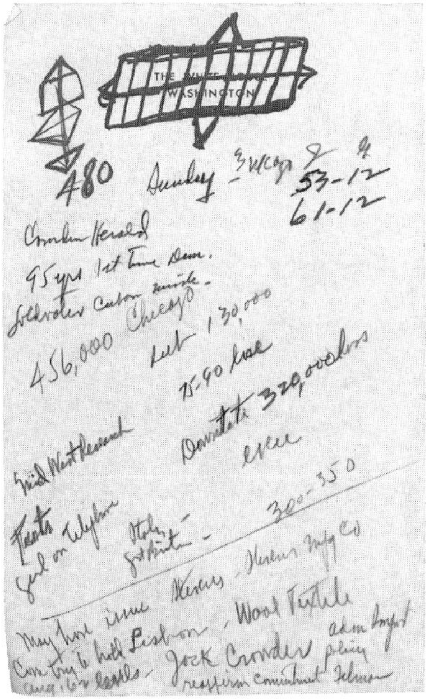
WASHINGTON
480
53-12
61-12
456,000
300-350
Jock Crowder

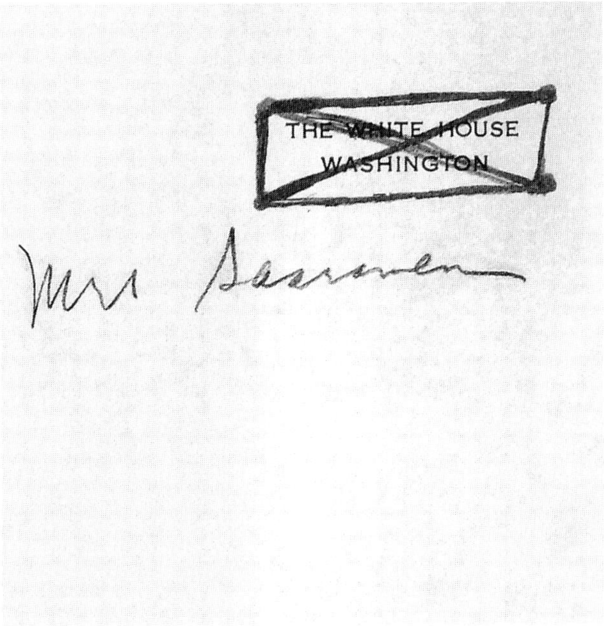
THE WHITE HOUSE
WASHINGTON

THE WHITE HOUSE
WASHINGTON

Chris draft reply Bt. Pm.

THE WHITE HOUSE

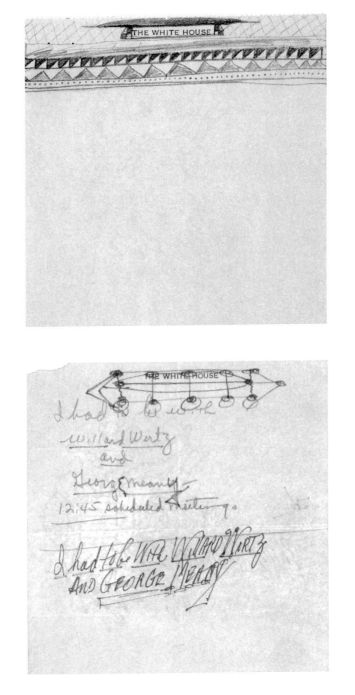

Johnson drew this doodle on August 11, 1964, just a week after the Gulf of Tonkin incident, which led to the escalation of the American military involvement in Vietnam. Clearly, LBJ had much on his mind. His notes include a reference to Barry Goldwater, his rival in the presidential race that year, and also a reminder to "answer [Adam] Yarmolinsky," an aide to Attorney General Robert Kennedy. An Oldsmobile and a Pontiac make appearances as well.

The word "breakdown" here probably refers to something innocent, such as a breakdown in communication. But it's hard not to read it and think of the terrible emotional toll Vietnam took on Johnson. No one has suggested that the president literally had a nervous breakdown, but he became increasingly anguished as the quagmire of the war deepened—not only leading to the deaths of many more American boys than he'd ever envisioned, but also constraining Johnson from fulfilling his vision of the Great Society. Richard Goodwin, a Kennedy aide who stayed on the White House staff into the Johnson administration, later wrote that he believed LBJ was suffering at the end from bouts of paranoid delusion—a claim, it should be noted, other Johnson aides vigorously denied.

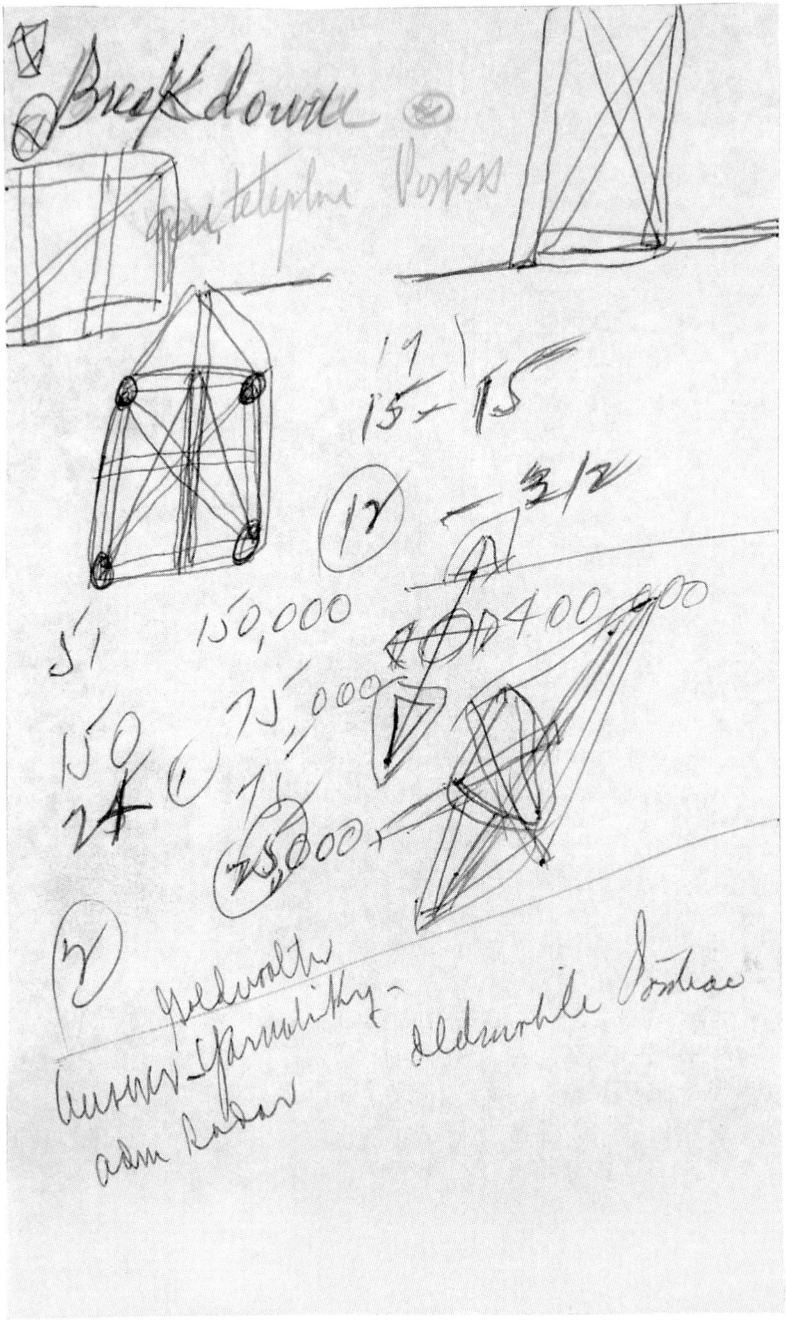
Breakdown
15 — 15
150,000
75,000
25,000
Goldwater
Oldsmobile Pontiac

ABC

abc
abcdefghijklmnopqrstuvwxyz

ABCDEFGHIJKLMNOPQ
RSTUVWXYZ.

This doodle comes from a meeting LBJ held with union and railroad leaders before an expected strike in April 1964. In addition to drawings of what look like a log cabin and split rail fences (and perhaps a tennis net), Johnson wrote the alphabet, as he was wont to do. Usually, however, LBJ generally didn't simply write out the alphabet from *A* to *Z* but rather repeated certain sequences of letters over and over. In a different picture he drew, it took him sixty-one letters to get to *Z* because of all his repetitions and backtracking.

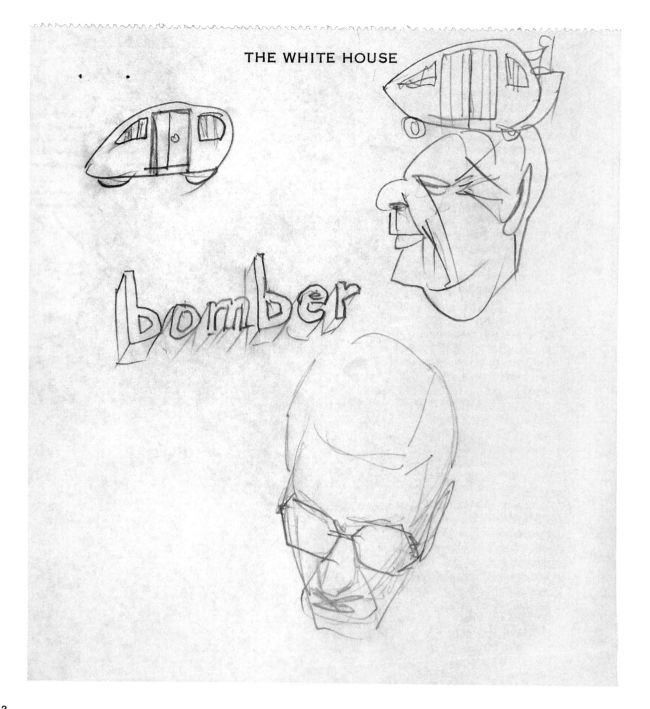

bomber

This doodle, and the ones on the next four pages, were made not by Johnson but by an unidentified White House guest over a few days in December 1964 when British Prime Minister Harold Wilson was visiting Washington. The subjects drawn by this mysterious doodler resemble Vice President Hubert Humphrey, Senator Edward M. Kennedy of Massachusetts, and other American and British officials.

Regardless of the artist's identity, it's clear that the Johnson White House was a hospitable home for doodlers.

Reflecting the rampant doodling in the Johnson White House, this drawing appears to be a hybrid of two different scribblers' work. The frieze drawn around "The White House" on the stationery may very well be the president's handiwork, but the cartoon creature below it is drawn in a different style.

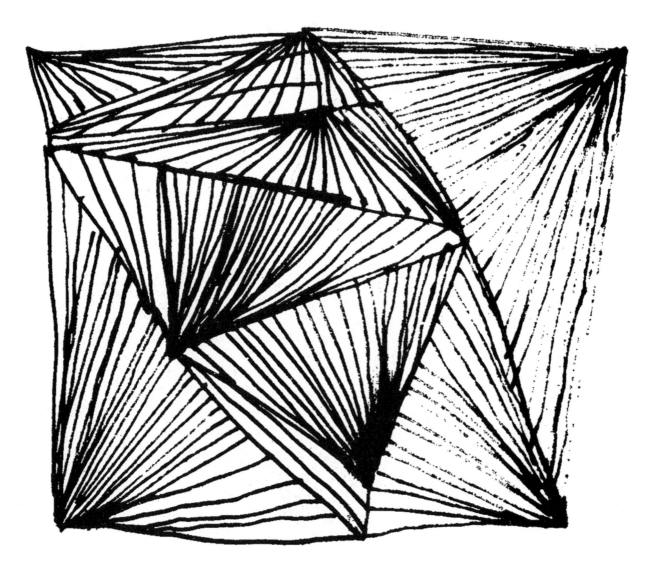

RICHARD NIXON
1969–1974

IT'S NOT SURPRISING that Richard Nixon didn't doodle much given how inhibited he was. Or perhaps he doodled but, in true Nixonian fashion, destroyed the drawings he made for fear that they might somehow incriminate him. He certainly doodled a bit, and he once described himself as "probably a square doodler." "I draw squares and diamonds and that sort of thing," he said to Frank Gannon, a post-presidential ghostwriter.

Nixon's most impressive artwork was a geometric shape drawn in response to a request from doodle compiler Norman Uris. The diamond-like sketch clearly shows the influence of the masterworks of Herbert Hoover–who had been a friend and mentor to Nixon since they met in 1950 at Northern California's Bohemian Grove club, a retreat for businessmen and politicians.

When William Safire was writing his memoir of his years as a Nixon speech-writer, he managed to obtain doodles from presidential aides including John Ehrlichman and Elliott Richardson. Safire mentioned his growing collection to Nixon's chief of staff, H. R. Haldeman, in hopes of soliciting one from the president. "I know what you're getting at," Haldeman interjected. "The president does not doodle" (obviously a falsehood, given the evidence presented here). Then, noted Safire, Haldeman shot the speechwriter a glare "with a humorously evil expression that spoke volumes about his understanding of image merchants in the throes of manipulation." Inquired the chief of staff: "*Should* the president doodle?"

REVISED AGENDA

CABINET COMMITTEE ON ECONOMIC POLICY
March 7, 1969, 10:45
Cabinet Room

1. The unemployment-inflation problem.

-- Paul W. McCracken

-- George P. Shultz

2. Voluntary approach to price stability.

-- Herbert Stein

3. Inter-agency study of agricultural exports.

-- Clifford M. Hardin

-- Hendrik S. Houthakker

4. Study of Government Programs with direct price-cost effects.

-- Paul W. McCracken

5. Lumber supply and prices.

-- Hendrik S. Houthakker

6. Investment controls.

-- David M. Kennedy

-- Maurice H. Stans

2

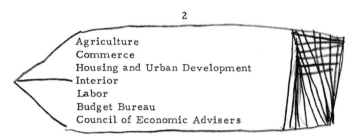

Agriculture
Commerce
Housing and Urban Development
Interior
Labor
Budget Bureau
Council of Economic Advisers

[It seems appropriate that either the Budget Bureau or the Council of Economic Advisers will coordinate the work.]

An interim report should be presented to the Cabinet Committee by April 15 and a final report by May 31.

Paul W. McCracken

"I always watch my opposite numbers to see how they doodle," Nixon told Frank Gannon—and he surely considered the possibility that his opposite numbers did likewise. "I noticed that, for example, in 1972, when we were having our first discussion with Brezhnev about missiles. We—the argument was as to whether or not a big missile could be put in a smaller hole. . . . While we were talking about it, he would draw holes and then missiles . . . to see whether or not they could go in the holes and so forth and so on. And down here, when we were meeting in a cabaña looking out over the Black Sea, he doodled—in this case, he drew a heart with an arrow through it. I don't know what that signified, but that was when we were failing to reach agreement on a proposal to limit MIRVs [multiple independently targeted reentry vehicles, or nuclear warheads], which we had proposed and which they had rejected—rejected, at least, on any meaningful basis."

RONALD REAGAN
1981–1989

BORN IN 1911, Ronald Reagan devoted most of his prepresidential career to mastering the modern media: radio, movies, television. His speaking and acting skills helped him convey sincerity as he evoked with his rhetoric a host of archetypal American images: the New England village and the Western frontier, high-school football games and small-town churches, neighborly values and rural innocence.

Reagan's kitschy doodles–most often, cartoon renderings of himself as a bandanna-wearing cowboy, a leather-helmeted running back in a 1930s pose, or simply a rugged leading man–likewise trigger a stream of warm, familiar associations with an idyllic American past. No less genuine because of their contrivance, they reveal Reagan's innate gift for political mythmaking.

Yet despite the prevalence of mythic tough guys, not all of Reagan's doodles reflect the Rambo image he created for himself. Many reveal a distinct aesthetic of cuteness. Reagan liked to draw babies and horses, showed a fondness for furry animals in the greetings cards he sent, and was not afraid to use gooey terms of endearment when writing to Nancy.

Reagan took great pride in his doodling. He had enjoyed drawing since he was a boy and as a young man considered a career as a cartoonist. He remained a lifelong fan of the comic strips. As he wrote to the political cartoonist Jeff MacNelly in 1984, "I am a cartoon aficionado up to and including reading the complete comics every morning. Along with that comes the editorial page for the cartoons–not the editorials."

Charles Schulz's "Peanuts," starring Snoopy and Charlie Brown, was one of Reagan's favorites. On May 24, 1967, as governor of California, he declared a Charles Schulz day, welcoming Snoopy's creator to the State Capitol. The Charles Schulz museum in Santa Rosa, California, boasts a fan letter to the cartoonist from Reagan that includes the president's trademark cowboy doodle of himself.

Having doodled throughout his life, Reagan frequently gave his drawings to colleagues, friends, and fans. One sold at auction in 1986 for $10,000.

Where James Garfield and Theodore Roosevelt drew bubbly, child-centric doodles, Reagan wrote adoring love notes to his wife. By turns playful and juvenile, affecting and cloying, they seem like the mash notes of a teenager in the throes of puppy love.

The figure at the bottom in the center is probably Nancy Reagan. The First Lady had this page framed and kept it on her desk.

Even during his days as governor of California (and probably earlier), Reagan drew pages full of the same cartoon figures. Just as professional cartoonists master a handful of regular characters for their strips, so Reagan developed a repertoire of favorite images. They recur again and again in what he called "collages" or galleries, like this one from 1970. While demonstrating an undeniable basic proficiency, they also seem highly stylized. One almost expects to see written underneath, "If you can draw this, you can go to art school."

Interestingly, Reagan had trouble drawing limbs such as hands, legs, and horses' hooves. Some psychobiographers have had a field day with this recurring omission, reading it as a sign of castration anxiety. Such Freudian interpretations aside, amputation was a theme in Reagan's cinematic career. In *The Girl from Jones Beach* (1949), he played a commercial illustrator who invents a fantasy pinup from the body parts of a dozen real women. In *Kings Row* (1942), he plays Drake McHugh, whose leg is needlessly amputated by the cruel father of his romantic interest. When Drake awakens to find his leg gone, he asks in horror, "Where's the rest of me?" Reagan used the phrase as the title of his first autobiography.

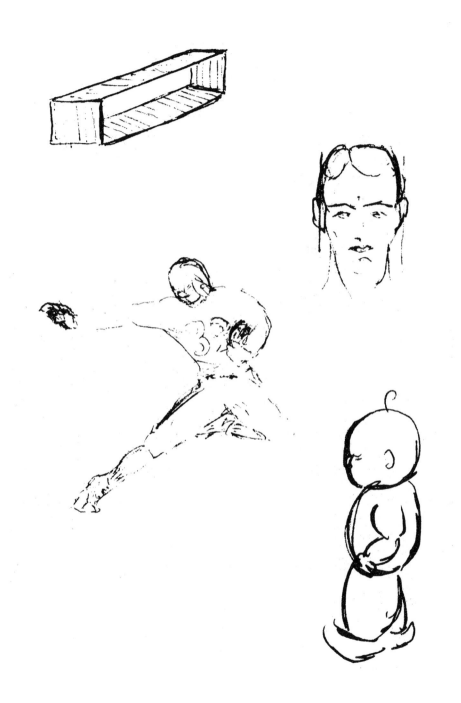

Dear Buggs
Here are some doodles
just to show I'm not
always busy.
Best Regards
Ronald Reagan

Although we think of doodling as the ultimate private act–drawing done without premeditation or even full awareness–Reagan clearly realized that his habit had public relations value. A White House photographer carefully snapped shots of each and every one of his characters, and toward the end of his presidency, a staffer compiled many of the drawings in a scrapbook.

The White House also happily allowed the drawings to be featured in the news media. *Time* magazine and the *CBS Evening News* ran stories about Reagan's doodles. "Although it may be flattering for someone who's talked with Mr. Reagan to receive an autographed presidential doodle, anyone who gets a horse or a football player had better watch out," reported Bill Plante on CBS. "Mr. Reagan doesn't do horses or football players, according to a longtime associate, unless what he's been listening to is really boring."

THE WHITE HOUSE

WASHINGTON

May 2, 1983

Dear Justin:

<u>Thank you very much for your drawings of the
Owl and the Puma Cub</u>. They are excellent.
I'm just a doodler but I recognize quality
work when I see it and yours is that.

Thanks again and give my regards to your
parents.

Sincerely,

Ronald Reagan

✗
Justin Murdock
10744 Bellagio Road
Los Angeles, California 90024

a doodle

Reagan sent his cartoons to his numerous pen pals, too, including one to "Buzzy" (page 194) and one to a young correspondent with artistic aspirations (opposite).

Nancy wrote in her book *I Love You, Ronnie* that her husband wrote her letters "all the time, including on ordinary days and sometimes more than once a day." She said she turned to his notes and drawings for sustenance when he was afflicted by Alzheimer's disease.

The Reagan estate has graciously allowed the following notes from Ronnie to Nancy to be published on the condition that they be printed with no accompanying commentary.

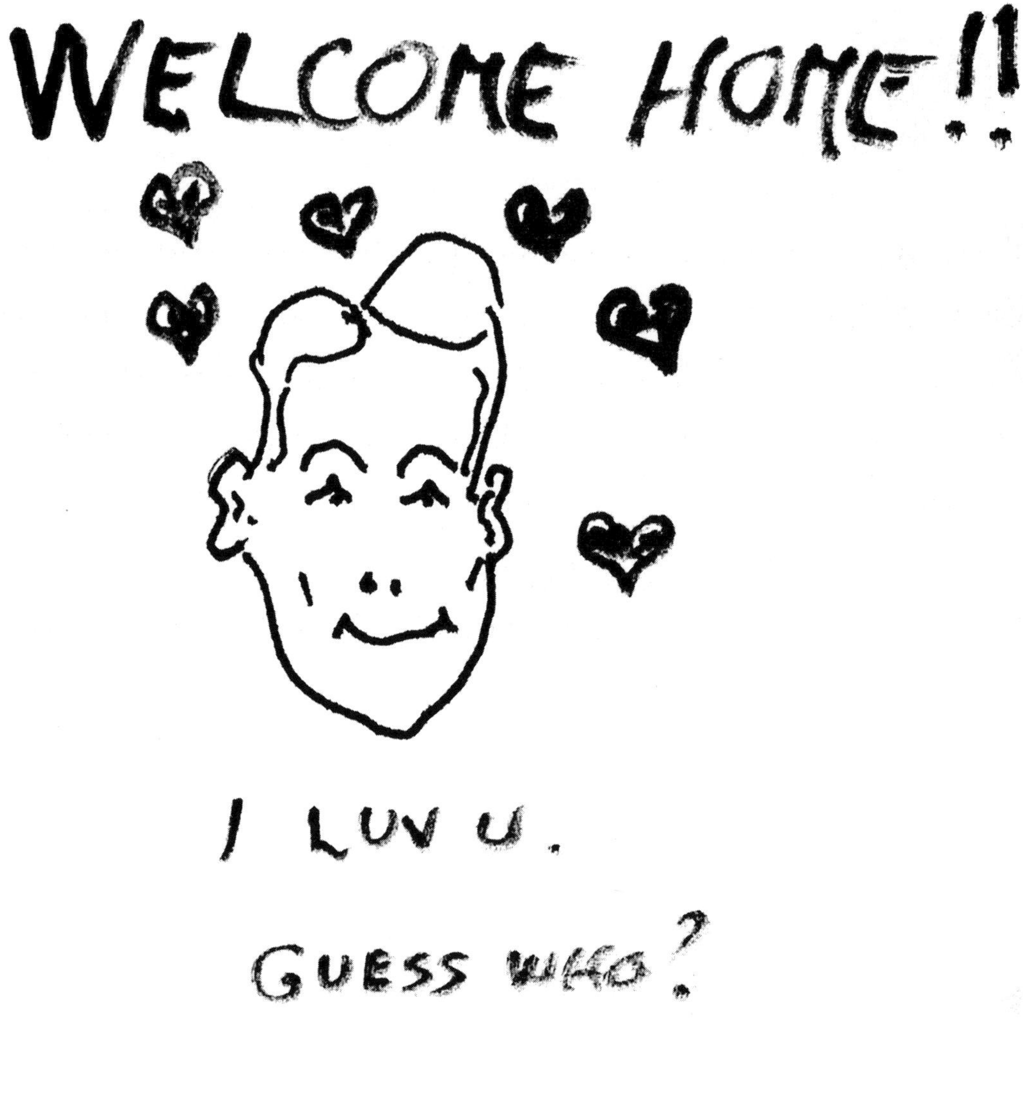
WELCOME HOME!!
I LUV U.
GUESS WHO?

THE WHITE HOUSE

Dear Mommie, Poo Pants, 1st Lady, Nancy
(How did I get so many wives?) Nevermind I
love them each & every one. I know it's only
Feb. 4th. — not Feb. 14th & not March 4th. —
but I can't stand it any longer. Happy
Valentines day !! Happy Anniversary !!
I Love You
Poppa, Poo Pants, 1st Guy, Ronnie

I Luv U + Missed a
Good Morning Kiss —

SMACK !!!

GUV

Dearest Mommie Poo

From your head to your toes
You're a wonderful wife--
And my love for you grows
Every day of my life !

HAPPY MOTHER'S DAY,
HONEY

(It may be Mother's Day
to them but it's Mommie Day
to me.)

I Love You
Poppa

IF THIS GETS INTO THE HANDS OF THE RUSSIANS, IT'S CURTAINS FOR THE FREE WORLD.

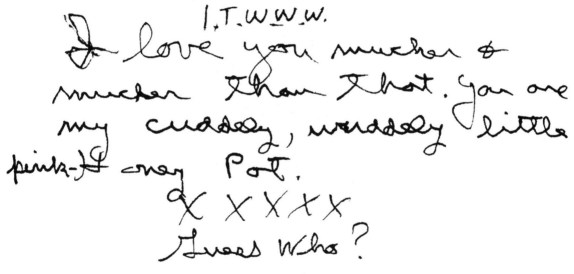

I,T,W,W,W.
I love you mucher & mucher than that. You are my cuddely, wuddely little pink-t oney Pot.
X X X X X
Guess Who?

Reagan's predilection for doodling faces, people, and animals was, at least according to one story, unusual for Republicans. The conservative journalist David Horowitz recounted an incident in which Reagan attended a meeting that included both Democrats and Republicans. A reporter who gathered up the doodles from both sides afterward found that all the Democrats had drawn animals and people's faces, while the Republicans had drawn geometric shapes. There was one exception: Reagan. Of course, Reagan had been a Democrat until the 1950s.

The isolated face at the bottom of this July 21, 1987, memo was not one of Reagan's usual doodles. When White House staffers discovered the drawing, they asked the president about it. According to Kathy Osborne, Reagan's personal secretary, Reagan said that "he was making sure his pen was working by making a scribble mark on the page. Then he realized this page would be reviewed by archivists and researchers in the future. He didn't want to be viewed as messy so he created the doodle not to represent anyone but to be less 'messy.'"

The President has seen 7/21

THE SCHEDULE OF PRESIDENT RONALD REAGAN

Tuesday, July 21, 1987

9:00 am (30 min)	Staff Time (Vice President/Baker/Duberstein)		Oval Office
9:30 am (60 min)	Meeting with GOP Congressional Leadership (Ball)	(TAB A)	Cabinet Room
10:30 am (30 min)	National Security Briefing (Carlucci)		Oval Office
11:00 am (15 min)	Senior Staff Time		Oval Office
11:15 am (45 min)	Personal Staff Time		Oval Office
12:00 m (90 min)	Lunch and Personal Staff Time		Oval Office
1:30 pm (15 min)	Take Pride in America Event (Risque)	(TAB B)	Rose Garden
2:00 pm (2 hrs)	Personal Staff Time		Oval Office
4:00 pm (30 min)	Meeting with Secretary Weinberger		Oval Office

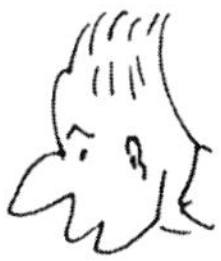

UNP 07/20/87
4:00 pm

In late 1986, news surfaced that the Reagan administration had sold arms to Iran for the release of American hostages, and that proceeds from the sale were used illegally to fund the Nicaraguan contras fighting against the left-wing regime there. A key issue in the probe into "Iran-contra" was the question of how much Reagan knew about what was going on around him. Some administration officials, such as National Security Council aide Oliver North, admitted that they had shredded documents as part of a cover-up. When investigators sought to obtain Reagan's own papers, the cartoonist Tom Toles imagined what they might turn up.

Rose

1 confirmed
dead
==

1 possible dead
→

How bout all
the rest? Any
more dead ons?

GEORGE H. W. BUSH

1989–1993

THE 1978 PRESIDENTIAL Records Act declared any records documenting the president's constitutional, statutory, or ceremonial duties to be public property. As a result, several of Ronald Reagan's doodles are open to the public. George Bush, Sr., however, was extraordinarily secretive as president and used a provision in the 1978 law to designate vast swaths of papers as "privileged," including much material normally not recognized as such. As a result, daily agendas, memos, and other apparently routine White House paperwork remain off-limits to historians–and doodle hunters.

The one significant doodle-like drawing currently available in Bush's presidential papers appears on a memo he wrote to Rose Zamaria, his secretary. Was Bush distraught at the deaths of American servicemen? Miners trapped underground? An airplane crash? According to Zamaria, the sad face with tears that Bush made showed nothing of the sort. The president was responding to a request from her to sign a stack of letters–part of a mass mailing–addressed to people he knew. Looking over the names, Bush realized that one of the intended recipients was dead and that another one might be. "You see," explained Zamaria, "he was such a funny guy."

GEORGE W. BUSH
2001–PRESENT

NEITHER BILL CLINTON nor George W. Bush responded to requests for samples of their presidential doodles, and only a tiny portion of Clinton's presidential papers—and none of Bush's—are yet open to the public. But Bush did scrawl a note to Secretary of State Condoleezza Rice that, like the finest doodles, revealed him in an unguarded moment. At the United Nations in 2005, during a speech by the leader of Benin, Bush wrote to Rice, "I think I MAY NEED A BATHROOM break? Is this possible?" Reuters photographer Rick Wilking caught the note on film. (One might ask why a president who insisted he didn't need a permission slip *from* the UN to go to war felt he did need a permission slip *at* the UN to go to the bathroom.)

Not surprisingly, the president was chagrined to have the note made public. Although it's easy to mock, his private message did little more than express a basic human need. In these days of stage-managed politics, however, our eagerness to catch a glimpse of the unscripted president too often gets the better of us— whether that glimpse comes from a trivial note, a public gaffe, or an idly drawn but lovingly preserved presidential doodle.

EPILOGUE

Presidential Doodles began as a whimsical idea tossed out during a 2002 editorial meeting at *Cabinet* magazine: to gather and publish a small portfolio of doodles by some famous figures of the twentieth century. A quick preliminary search turned up exactly two inveterate doodlers–John F. Kennedy and Jack Kerouac. Although we could have spent the next several years searching for doodles by Kerouac and other literary stars, the chuckle-inducing collision of the words "president" and "doodle" had an immediate and irresistible appeal. We dropped Kerouac and focused on finding more doodlers-in-chief.

The research task we set out to accomplish–locate doodles by as many U.S. presidents as possible–was daunting but seemed straightforward. Beginning with Herbert Hoover, every president has a dedicated library administered by the National Archives and staffed by career archivists familiar with the holdings of the library. The records of earlier presidents are even more centralized; the vast majority are preserved in the Manuscript Division of the Library of Congress and have been microfilmed for easy research. Indeed, our first presidential library visit, to the Kennedy Library in 2002, was simple beyond belief: when we mentioned "doodles," the archivists nodded knowingly and led us to a large folder labeled as such. We simply flipped through the folder, marveling at JFK's bizarre word combinations and interlocking squares, and left with enough photocopies for an entire book.

We did not realize until later that Kennedy doodle research was an exception. Kennedy was known for his doodles–they had even been exhibited in 1964–and the files we browsed were well-thumbed. We found to our chagrin that few other presidential archives had such a conveniently labeled file. Equally rare was the mention of doodles in finding aids, the indexing tool that helps researchers navigate archival collections. A description of a set of papers could contain meticulously detailed information about the subject matter but fail to mention any accompanying graphics, no matter how much these dominated the page. At times, we caught a whiff of doodle discrimination that might have accounted for such striking omissions. An archivist once referred to one of our most sought-after doodles as "a bit of doggerel," and another wrote a bit too emphatically that indeed Carter made many notes but we could rest assured that they were all business. In the Eisenhower library, we found evidence that certain conspicuous doodles had been erased, perhaps by Eisenhower himself or maybe by an abashed archivist. Even more mysterious, our request to the William Clinton Foundation for doodles (we appealed directly to the foundation because the Clinton Presidential Library did not open to the public until 2006) was turned down by Clinton's press office. We can only speculate why.

Despite the intricacies and idiosyncrasies of various presidential archives, we soon amassed a sampling of drawings, ranging from the childish to the terrifying, by eight twentieth-century presidents. Novelist Jonathan Ames, himself an avid doodler, was invited to comment on a selection of these, and the portfolio was published in *Cabinet*'s Fall 2003 issue.

From the beginning, we had known that presidential doodles would be fascinating simply by virtue of our inexhaustible interest in our heads of state. What we had not anticipated were the complicated and subtle ways that these oddly intimate scribblings would expose the particular anxieties, issues, neuroses, and penchants of the doodling president. And so in 2004, we decided to expand our research and attempt to publish a book of doodles by all U.S. presidents, starting with Washington.

We had a mind-boggling amount of ground to cover. Each of the twelve presidential libraries houses millions of pieces of paper. The combined papers of all presidents before Hoover number in the area of two million manuscript pages–these range from 631 pieces in the case of Zachary Taylor to 500,000 in the case of William H. Taft. The size of the collection depends on many factors: whether the collection was damaged at any stage; to what extent papers were sold for profit or otherwise dispersed; whether the president took office before or after the invention of the copy machine; whether he instructed his secretaries or assistants to save *everything* or only things of a certain importance; and finally, whether the president was of a mind to destroy his papers on leaving office (a practice thankfully outlawed by the Presidential Records Act of 1978).

Chester Arthur is the most notorious case of a president bent on leaving no paper trail–the night before his death, Arthur burned three garbage pails of his papers, each four feet high. So thorough was the destruction that, for many years, the Library of Congress's Arthur Collection consisted of a single manuscript. In contrast, there were presidents like George Washington, who carefully removed his papers from New York City in 1776 in anticipation of a British attack; or Theodore Roosevelt, a historian and biographer himself, who put great stock in primary sources and preserved accordingly; or James Garfield, whose papers overflowed the house he had designed to accommodate them–papers were "corded up like firewood" even in the bathroom.

Some papers fell victim to purposeful destruction, but others were lost by unfortunate happenstance or carelessness. Ulysses S. Grant, for instance, was prone to misplacing papers (and even entire manuscripts), whereas James Madison liked to pass them on as gifts to his family. War took a great toll on many presidential paper collections. John Tyler's plantation was ransacked by the Union Army, as was the home of Zachary Taylor's son. In both cases, the plunder included invaluable papers that were destroyed or sold. When Confederates seized Andrew Johnson's Tennessee plantation in 1864, soldiers reported to their commanding colonel the presence of a large wooden box in Johnson's library. Knowing of Johnson's liking for aged rye whiskey, the colonel ordered that the box be brought to him immediately. To his disgust, he found it contained papers, not whiskey, and ordered that the contents be destroyed.

Of course, even if we had had access to every single piece of paper written on by every single president, we would not have found doodles by every one. Some presidents relieved their anxiety or boredom without putting pen to paper. Gerald Ford, for instance, did not doodle–he fiddled with his pipe. Others chewed their pens, bit their nails, rolled cigarettes, or chewed gum. Harry S. Truman doodled infrequently but was prone to counting down from ten to one in the margin of his notepad, each number aligned in a perfectly spaced grid. Some presidents simply avoided writing things altogether. William McKinley, for instance, was notoriously loath to write letters and preferred face-to-face conversation.

Every so often, a doodling president's collection was both large and well-organized, as is the case with the Lyndon B. Johnson Library, which houses hundreds of doodles. Although such an organized and bounteous collection as Johnson's was a godsend to our project, we could not help but be amused by the stacks of doodles meticulously collated, stapled, dated, and labeled "doodles from the president's bedroom," "doodles from the Oval Office coffee table," "doodles from Air Force One trip," and so on. We imagined a secretary who trailed the president all day long, scooping up every scrap of paper his hand touched and squirreling it away.

Of course, not all presidential papers are equally endowed with "doodle potential," and we soon outlined some guidelines to make our search more efficient. Folders labeled "miscellaneous items," "random notes," or "handwriting file" had the highest doodle potential. Next in line was the daily agenda, a piece of paper traditionally placed on the president's desk every morning. Notes made during cabinet meetings could be promising, as were speech drafts. Correspondence files contain lots of handwriting, but were usually a dead end for doodles. Our last resort–and a fruitful place to find drawings and sketches, if not doodles *per se*–were files containing juvenilia or school notebooks. If the president was a habitual doodler, we could afford to select only the most visually striking images. If we weren't finding anything, we would focus on certain days or months that might have been particularly stressful in the White House–our hypothesis being that a certain amount of anxiety or pressure would have spurred even a puritan nondoodler to emit an errant sketch.

To scan as many pieces of paper in as little time as possible, we also perfected a strategy of "distracted looking." When looking at microfilm, we set the machines at a speed fast enough that we couldn't read a single word, making it easier to notice any nonuniform script. This allowed us to cover about six reels– about nine thousand pieces of paper–per hour. The method induced something akin to car sickness, but we persevered, driven by our historic mission. When viewing paper records, we mechanically turned papers at a steady rhythm, replacing file with file, box with box, and cart with cart, as quickly but thoroughly as possible. Suffice to say, despite having spent several years in presidential archives, we have learned little of substance about any of the presidents.

Archivists were crucial to our search. Some were intrigued by the unusual research query; others were befuddled by our interest in what seemed to them a trivial subject; and still others were a bit defensive, as if they perceived a hidden insult in the question. But in all cases, their assistance was invaluable. They directed us toward promising files, advised with questions of authorship, deciphered illegible handwriting, and provided much-needed context. At presidential libraries far from home–in West Branch, Iowa, for example, or Austin, Texas–they also kindly recommended places to eat and things to do when the library closed.

The collection of images in this book comprises the best of our research. Of course, not every doodle drawn by our leaders has been included in *Presidential Doodles*. But the persistent preoccupations, the artistic skills or lack thereof, the startling obsessions, the meticulous drawings, and the harried, anxious marks are amply represented. Everything is here in all its trivial glory, and perhaps it is not so trivial after all.

Sasha Archibald and Sina Najafi
Cabinet magazine

ACKNOWLEDGMENTS

Cabinet magazine would like to thank Paul Collins, Jeffrey Cunard, David Greenberg, Carole Goodman, Ryo Manabe, and Michelle Tessler, without whom this book would still be a stack of photocopied doodles. Many others were crucial in the making of the book, including Jonathan Ames, Beth Baker, Gabrielle Begue, William L. Bird, Jr., Harold Dorwin, Kate Fox, Elizabeth Glennerster, Chelsea Goodchild, Jeffrey Kastner, Raymond Ku, Michelle Legro, Brian McMullen, Steve Rowell, Mark Santelgo, David Schwartz, Courtney Stephens, and Chaya Thanhauser. We will forever be indebted to the dedicated librarians, archivists and other staff members who patiently assisted us with our unorthodox research, especially Bonnie Cole at the Library of Congress Photoduplication Services, Barbara Constable at the Lyndon B. Johnson Presidential Library, Joanne Drake at the Ronald Reagan Foundation, Marcus Eckhardt at the Herbert Hoover Presidential Museum, Jim Leyerzapf at the Dwight D. Eisenhower Library, Stephen Plotkin at the John F. Kennedy Presidential Library, Matt Schaefer at the Herbert Hoover Presidential Library, and Randy Sowell at the Harry S. Truman Archive.

David Greenberg wishes to thank Jonathan Alter, Audrey Baker, Jill Barshay, Vin Cannato, Derek Chollet, Caleb Crain, Matt Dallek, Juliet Eilperin, Ann Fabian, Leslie Fishbein, Eric Foner, Joanne Freeman, Garance Franke-Ruta, Tom Glynn, Mitch Golden, Fred Greenstein, Hendrik Hertzberg, Zachary Karabell, Peter Kastor, Bob Kubey, Jan Lewis, Peter Matson and Sterling Lord Literistic, Tim Naftali, Michael Nelson, Roger Newman, Tim Noah, David Plotz, Tim Raphael, Barbara Reed, Matt Rees, Michael Rockland, Gary Rosen, Jonathan Schoenwald, Michael Schudson, Peter Scoblic, Josh Shenk, Jeff Shesol, Ben Sifuentes-Jáuregui, Michael Signer, Mark Alan Stamaty, Chris Suellentop, Margaret Talbot, Dan Tichenor, Gil Troy, Ellen Wu, and Emily Yoffe. And of course Judith and Ira, Jon and Megan, Mom and Dad, Renee, Deon, Ilana, and Jordan, and most of all Suzanne and Leo.

Cabinet and David Greenberg would like to thank Arthur Arundel, William Morrison Garland, Christine Marra, Tom Toles, Nikil Saval, and Kate Waldeck; Brandon Proia for his indispensable research; and especially Lara Heimert, our editor at Basic, who brought together this sprawling project and made it into a book.

ABOUT THE AUTHORS

SASHA ARCHIBALD and SINA NAJAFI are associate editor and editor-in-chief of *Cabinet* magazine, respectively. Described by the *New York Times* as "voracious, omnivorous, and playful," *Cabinet* is a nonprofit quarterly dedicated to creating a new culture of curiosity about the world.

DAVID GREENBERG is a professor of history and journalism at Rutgers University, and the author of the award-winning *Nixon's Shadow: The History of an Image.* A regular columnist for *Slate,* he has written for the *New York Times, Washington Post, New Yorker, Atlantic Monthly, Foreign Affairs,* and other scholarly and popular publications. A former managing editor and acting editor of the *New Republic,* he holds a B.A. from Yale and a Ph.D. in history from Columbia.

PAUL COLLINS is the author of *The Trouble With Tom: The Strange Afterlife and Times of Thomas Paine,* and the upcoming history *The Book of William: How Shakespeare's First Folio Conquered the World.* He edits the Collins Library for *McSweeney's Books,* and his work regularly appears in the *Village Voice* and *New Scientist.*